How to Raise a Man

THE MODERN MOTHER'S GUIDE TO PARENTING HER TEENAGE SON

Megan de Beyer

PENGUIN BOOKS

How to Raise a Man
Published by Penguin Books
an imprint of Penguin Random House (Pty) Ltd
Company Reg. No. 1953/000441/07
The Estuaries No. 4, Oxbow Crescent, Century Avenue, Century City, Cape Town, 7441
www.penguinrandomhouse.co.za

First published 2020
Reprinted in 2020

3 5 7 9 10 8 6 4 2

Publication © Penguin Books 2020
Text © Megan de Beyer 2020

Cover image © iStockphoto/miflippo
Sneakers: Designed by Eightonesix/Freepik

All rights reserved. No part of this publication may be reproduced,
stored in a retrieval system or transmitted, in any form or by any means,
electronic, mechanical, photocopying, recording or otherwise,
without the prior written permission of the copyright owners.

PUBLISHER: Marlene Fryer
MANAGING EDITOR: Ronel Richter-Herbert
EDITOR: Laetitia Sullivan
PROOFREADER: Ronel Richter-Herbert
COVER DESIGN: Monique Cleghorn
TEXT DESIGN: Ryan Africa
TYPESETTER: Ryan Africa/Monique van den Berg

Set in 11.5 pt on 15 pt Adobe Caslon

Printed by **novus** print, a Novus Holdings company

978 1 77609 495 0 (print)
978 1 77609 496 7 (ePub)

Contents

Foreword ix
Introduction: It's time to let go 1
How to use this book 6

PART 1
Chapter 1: What type of mom are you? 10
Chapter 2: How to have better parenting conversations 29
Chapter 3: What is conscious parenting? 52
Chapter 4: 7 steps to tackle any parenting problem 67
Chapter 5: Who is this boy?! Understanding the stages
　　　　　of development 83
Chapter 6: Things all boys must learn 92
Chapter 7: Crippling parenting mistakes you may be making ... 106
Chapter 8: Respect the bro rules 118
Chapter 9: You're old school! Time to change your parenting style ... 130

PART 2
Chapter 10: Handling anger (his and yours) 141
Chapter 11: Bad behaviour: rudeness, defiance, lying,
　　　　　 moods, silence 159
Chapter 12: Sex and hook-ups on the brain 172
Chapter 13: Alcohol: The teen drug of choice 185
Chapter 14: Addiction issues and suicide 194
Chapter 15: Screens, porn and sexting 208
Chapter 16: Real issues that moms have 217

Final thoughts 226
Parent resources 231
Acknowledgements 235

For my sons, James and Jo.

'Anything or anyone that does not bring you alive is too small for you.' – *David Whyte*

Foreword

If there ever was a time and a need for a book called *How to Raise a Man* – not a *good* man; not a *decent* man; not *a man I wouldn't mind my daughter (or son) spending the rest of their life with*; just a *man*, unadorned – it's now.

The word 'man' once stood for very good things: strength, loyalty, bravery, dignity, morality. The best men were providers and their family's trusted heroes; the type who would rise from bed in the dead of night to investigate terrifying thumps and thuds in the dark. These days, it seems *men* are the terrifying thumps and thuds in the dark. Women fear them. We walk faster because of them, from the bus or taxi to the light, or as we turn down badly lit alleys, reaching for our pepper spray. We wonder whether we're safe when they pass us a drink in a club or stop us in the street. We fear them in the 'safety' of our homes: when their dinner is late on the table; when they're drinking; when their team loses, and when it wins. We worry about the safety of our daughters when men and boys come knocking at the door or rev their engines as they idle in the road outside.

And men suffer at the hands of other men, too.

And yet, as mothers, we know that among these men are our boys. Our adored, strong and gentle boys. The fact that good men seem to be teetering on the endangered species list is a shameful reality that needs to be discussed.

In this era of #metoo and #allmenaretrash, it's evident that something is going wrong with the way men emerge from childhood into their teenage years and beyond. As most children are brought up by women (whether in single-parent homes or not), it's easy to blame mothers. But toxic masculinity is a nasty, poisonous stew stirred by many hands. The task and responsibility of women raising boys is to bring up good men despite of it.

To succeed, we need help. It is a particularly cruel irony that as women are forced to confront the humbling, scary and confidence-sapping reality of aging and menopause, we are called upon to be role models for our adolescent children. If there is a god, he or she has a dark sense of humour.

As mothers, our children's need for us to be strong, purposeful and confident is urgent. They desperately need us to be able to establish boundaries, teach consequences, instil bravery, and educate them in the concept of right and wrong, especially during their tumultuous adolescent years. The combination of an insecure, unhappy mother and *any* teenager – let alone a rebellious, fragile or unhappy one – is not destined for success.

As we enter the third decade of the 21st century, the generational divide seems more treacherous and dizzying than ever before. Today, as parents, we have the added complication of trying to lead our families while teetering on a tightrope over the chasm of the digital revolution. Never before have humans been so bombarded with content, stimulation and temptation. We might use 'in my day' as a moral lodestar, but it is a faint echo from another time, increasingly unrecognisable both to our children and ourselves. Old rules and old methods don't work in this foreign environment. We are truly in uncharted territory. So how do we find certainty, confidence and joy in parenting modern boys? Well, we must ask for help.

Now, more than ever, we need to heed the old maxim, 'It takes a village to raise a child'. We cannot find support by believing it is our role to be all things to our children. Trying to be a child's 'everything' is an endeavour doomed to fail. Parenting is a journey best undertaken in a team. We need the wisdom of our communities; women were never intended to raise a child alone. We need shared knowledge, we need to know we're not alone, and we need the insight and expertise of professionals.

One of the greatest gifts a parent can bestow on a child is seeking psychological support for the family. This is a powerful weapon against the kind of misery that sad, lost, unparented children and angry, frustrated parents suffer.

Many hundreds of parents – myself included – can count themselves lucky to have called upon Megan de Beyer. Through her private practice in Cape Town and highly regarded Strong Mothers – Strong Sons workshops, Megan has supported hundreds of parents along the long and winding road to raising strong, decent men, helping women forge stronger bonds and closer understanding with their boys, and assisting them in navigating and coping with crises.

FOREWORD

In How to Raise a Man, Megan shares her experience and expertise in raising her own two boys, packaging her knowledge into a comprehensive and useful workbook that I believe will become the go-to guide for parents of teenage boys. The book guides mothers through questions to ask and conversations to have. It offers practical solutions and a programme to follow when parents feel lost. It offers advice that will strengthen resolve and empower mothers and fathers to be the kind of parents they want to be. It's not, as Megan says, about 'sloppy, smothering love', but about finding a love language that can instil confidence in order to raise a man who is strong enough to do the right thing, independent enough to forge his own path, and well-parented enough to become the contributor to society we all so desperately need him to be.

VANESSA RAPHAELY
Author, media consultant and founder of The Village, South Africa's happiest parenting social media community

Introduction:
It's time to let go

'Parenting is a mirror in which we get to see the best of ourselves, and the worst; the richest moments of living, and the most frightening.'

– Jon and Myla Kabat-Zinn, *Everyday Blessings: The Inner Work of Mindful Parenting*, 2011

One of the toughest moments in my life was when my youngest son told me, at age thirteen, that he wanted to go to boarding school. He had a way of stating things as if they were final. Not a question or a suggestion – this was something he had 100 per cent decided. I was mortified and plagued with guilt, and felt totally rejected.

I was also in denial at the time.

I was a single mom, working full-time, often late to pick him up from sports after school, and got into bad moods with the evening traffic back home. On top of this, my two sons and I were all dating! Logically, my son was highlighting the clash of schedules and that I was not yet integrating the real difficulties of being a single working mom raising two teen boys. His words stung. He was telling me that he needed independence and wanted a more male environment.

Everything in me wanted to hold on, change my schedule, spend more time with him ... But that's not what he wanted. There was no way *he* wanted to spend more time with *me*. I was regressing and wishing for the past, while he was progressing. He had already made it clear that although he loved mountain biking, he was not about to bike with me on my own. That was boring!

When my sons were about fifteen and sixteen, I found myself in conversations with other moms: What had happened to our sweet boys? The ones we cuddled and who thought we were the best?

I was a psychologist who'd worked with children and parents for years, and I was as baffled and hurt as the other moms were. It seemed as if, overnight, our sons had become hypercritical and rejecting:

'Don't drop me at the gate.'

'Why are you wearing that dress?'

'Chill, Mom!'

Our boys were responding to us in monosyllables and sometimes with contempt – if they responded at all. Our relationship seemed a tenuous thing.

Don't feel smug if your younger teen isn't showing these signs yet.

He will.

Then you will set out with good intentions to have a decent conversation with him. You will clear your mind and soften your heart, and you will say, 'Darling, let's talk about the holidays/next week/your relationship with your dad …'

And the shutters will come down. As if a big roller-blind fell down between you and him.

He's zoned you out!

He's either saying it directly to you, or he's doing it by his withdrawal and silence, rolling his eyes or looking at his phone.

Our boys are irritated with us, with their siblings, with other family members … They are even fighting with their friends. We start to see behaviour we don't approve of. They are often bad-tempered, slamming doors, swearing, rolling their eyes. And that's when they bother to look up from their phones.

Gone are the days of:

'Mommy, Mommy, look how high I can climb!'

'Mommy, Mommy, time me as I run up the stairs!'

'Mommy, Mommy, look at this painting and please put it on the wall.'

Where was the boy who couldn't wait for you to get home so that you could spend time together, to hug and tumble on the bed and read books?

Gone forever.

Sorry.

I suggested to my friends that I put together a workshop where we could come together and try to understand what was going on, to find a path that would strengthen our relationships with our sons, while still holding true to the values of our homes. That was over a decade ago.

That first workshop I ran, with then school counsellor Jason Bantjes, called Strong Mothers – Strong Sons, began with questions around masculinity, and thoughts about how we mothers (beings of oestrogen and progesterone) could best address the changes testosterone was wreaking in our sons. I found that I had hit on an area that parents were very concerned about.

In no time, the workshop became a course and began its own journey. The course has been to every major city in South Africa, and has travelled to California, the UK and Australia. I've also been invited to take it to Ghana, Namibia, Zambia and Botswana.

Part of its remarkable success is because the programme has been built around the questions that mothers asked me at that first workshop, and have asked me since – in the emails that I have received, and from the hundreds of queries sent to me as an expert on parenting.

My well-adjusted adult sons are also a source of inspiration, reminding me what helped or hindered them during their growth to maturity.

But it's not only the input of parents that has informed (and formed) the content for my Strong Mothers – Strong Sons course and this book. The programme also incorporates insights from older teen boys. This adds another dimension that grounds the advice and information given in absolute authenticity.

For more than a decade, at every school I have visited, I have interviewed a group of senior boys in their final year (generally age seventeen or eighteen). So I know what boys think, do and want! And I am here to share that.

From these interviews, it became clear that some things needed unpacking:
1. Mothers don't understand the male teen process and the developmental phases ALL boys will go through. Only when you understand this can you place your teen's behaviour in context.
2. How you mother a teenager has to be very different from how you mother a little boy. Clearly, what had worked when they were little is not working now, and will set you on a collision course.
3. Mothers are women and not men. The unfolding of masculinity involves different rites of passage and hormones than becoming a woman.
4. Mothers are either blaming themselves or blaming their teen for conflict.
5. Mothers need more self-awareness, and they need a philosophy of parenting that they believe in.

Mothering a teen can be an anxious time. We are preparing our boys to live in the world, to create a life and to find a space for themselves. We do our best to help them develop their personalities, their skills and their wholeness. We see ourselves as guardians of their lives and spirits and hearts. We want to be sure that we have handed over all the skills, knowledge and love that will help them move forward in their own lives. We want to be sure that our relationship with them will be strong enough so that, when they go into the world, their love will bring them back (now and again, or as often as possible!) to the family, or at least to their foundational values.

These instincts are right: a teen boy's relationship with his parents is vital, because it is what will inoculate him against all the vices out there. If he values his relationship with you, his relationship with his father and with his home, it is in his mind when he is making those impulsive, sometimes unsafe, decisions. In saying this, I always add a proviso – IF there is not an underlying mental health condition.

If the shutdown hasn't happened to you yet, don't worry.

It will.

It will make you angry.

It will break your heart.

You will feel like you've lost him.

But there is something the hundreds of senior boys I've spoken to all say, and moms need to hear this. It is the most important gift I can give you. Whatever is going on in your home right now, no matter how challenging, no matter how difficult, no matter how much your son seems to be turning on you or not speaking to you, know that he loves you with all his heart. You are the beacon of unconditional love for him, and you are one of the most important anchors in his life. Yes, even in those moments when you are standing there thinking, 'What have I done wrong? What's going on here? How can I improve?'

The main aim of this book is to help you survive the teens with your sanity intact and, in the process, discover that side of you that is an open-hearted adult. But it is more than that. It is to show you how to build a new relationship with your teenage son (and not become a copycat teen in the process). Teens are the ones who overreact, sulk, withdraw or blame.

All the information and exercises in the book are to help you find ways to have a deeper connection, so that you are able to create a sanctuary from

INTRODUCTION: IT'S TIME TO LET GO

the world out there. We all have that as a vision – our home as a sanctuary, a place you and your family go to for safety. Since the first print, Covid-19 has broken out and become a global pandemic. My words ring more true than ever. Our priorities have been radically impacted. Having good relationships and keeping family close is more urgent than ever.

Strong Mothers – Strong Sons was never a 'perfect mother' course. Far from it. It is about discovering yourself in your role as a mother to a teen boy. The prime principle of the course and this book is to teach you how to show up, and in what manner to show up, with as much openness and availability as you can muster amid the realities of life, the chores that you have and the work that you have to complete.

My boys have now been through university, and have embarked on their careers. The first time my older son took me to lunch and paid with his credit card, I couldn't believe it.

It may be hard for you to imagine that the day will arrive when you are not stretching yourself to your limits to cover all the costs – emotional as well as financial – that raising boys require. The time between ages thirteen and eighteen moves incredibly fast. That's just five birthdays! If your son has already turned fourteen, you're down to four. We have to make the most of the time we have with them. And, as I realised all those years ago, parenting a teenager is very different from mothering a little boy.

Happy mothering! May you become a wise teacher and a willing student. Prioritise what is most essential: relaxed time together without an agenda.

MEGAN

How to use this book

While you read this book, focus on bringing curiosity to the time you spend reading it, but also in the moments when you're doing other things – particularly when interacting with your son. Do not allow judgement to creep in while you observe yourself. Just be curious. Yes, you are going to learn a lot about what your son is going through, but you will also learn a lot about yourself. The course this book is based on is called Strong Mothers – Strong Sons, not simply 'Strong Sons'. Go gently on yourself, and just be curious about who you are in the parenting role.

Don't worry: I guarantee that by the end of this book, mothers of even the most monosyllabic teens will have had a meaningful conversation with their son. It's a promise I make in the first session of my course, and I've never had to eat my words. The course and the tools I present really work. This has been proven year in and year out, and has resulted in stronger relationships, better lines of communication, and a deeper understanding of your son, of yourself and your place in his life. You will never again settle for the crumbs of his attention. You will be empowered, and he will be more accountable for his actions.

At the end of every chapter, you'll find some of the exercises I ask moms on the course to do, either in the course, or at home before the next session. They are an important part of the programme, so don't skip them to get to the next chapter. Any therapist will tell you that therapy is not about what happens in the therapist's rooms, but what happens outside them. Buy a journal or use your device to write down the responses to all the questions asked. Then apply what you've learnt.

Giving you information is not the magic that causes a shift or movement in your relationship with your son. It's the actual time spent and the manner in which you spend that time with your family that makes the difference.

It's about how much you are 'leaning in' and engaging, as opposed to just being out there doing your own thing and letting him do his own thing:

What is your attitude?
How are you in the home?
How available and present are you?

It's the actual experience of parent-*ing* in the moment that is important, not the thinking about parenting, not the reading about parenting, not the taking in of information. While you read this book, be curious and monitor how you are in your home with your children. (I also believe we should be saying my son is teenage-*ing* and not that he is a teenager. It's an active and dynamic process that unfolds in stages and not a static state he reaches.)

I know that you want some practical solutions and techniques, and those are included in this book, too. We are also going to look at YOU. **Parenting allows us to discover the best or worst versions of ourselves**. That is why I call parenting a 'sacred practice'. Anything that moves you to be more empathetic, vulnerable, authentic or loving in your approach to another is a sacred practice. Gaining insight into yourself shifts consciousness, which ushers in effortless change.

At the heart of all the world's religions is a message inspiring us to be more loving and open human beings, who are meaningfully connected to each other. I do believe in a spirituality of the heart that promotes the development of a loving and whole person, and this is what parenting does for us. It gives us the opportunity for our own daily spiritual practice.

This programme is not about soft, sloppy, smothering love. It's all about that fierce love that makes you want to parent in an effective but not controlling way, to create a platform for your son to be the best he can be; a fierce love that recognises that being 'soft and permissive', allowing him to do what he wants, will not be effective in raising a fine young man.

A quick warning … If your son sees this book, his first thought is going to be that this means problems for him. His second thought might be, 'It's going to get stricter around here.' The third thing he'll assume is that you are reading this book because you think there is something wrong with him.

Tell him the truth! You are reading this book for yourself. You're reading it to work out what teenagers need from their parents. You are excited about self-growth and learning, about discovering and enriching yourself. It is important that you have this conversation with your son, otherwise he could resist everything you attempt as a result of what you read here.

PART 1

*'It takes so long to learn to take
your place in your own life.'*

– Ingeborg Bachmann

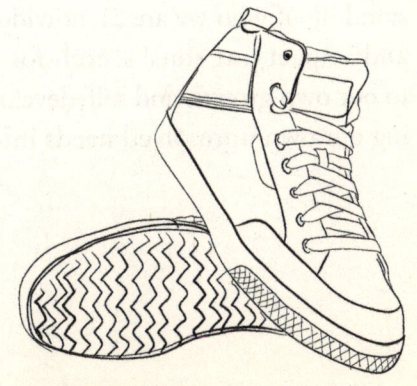

CHAPTER 1

What type of mom are you?

'Your teen needs you to be a Wise and Empowered Mom. Where are you now?'

To become an empowered mother, it is necessary to reflect on yourself as an individual and ask the most critical question:
'Who am I?'

Your teenager is going through the most profound process in the human life cycle, as it involves all levels of development: physical, cognitive, social, emotional and spiritual. The developmental psychologist Erik Erikson tells us that a boy in this phase is going through the psychosocial stage of identity formation and individuation.

Your teen is pulling away from his parents, especially his mother, to discover his masculine sense of self, separate from his family. He is seeking his identity and who he is apart from those he has always been dependent on. On a physical level, he is packed with male hormones that alter his view of girls and, possibly, his mother. It makes sense then that, if we as mothers are to assist our sons and maintain an interdependent, healthy relationship, we need to be empowered mothers.

This requires knowing ourselves and, at least, having a general understanding of who we are as individuals, and how that will affect our mothering and impact our sons' search for their identity. It requires a commitment to our own growth and self-development, so that we become aware of dumping our own unresolved needs into the mix.

TYPES OF MOMS

Let's look at some ideas of core beliefs that may be underlying many reactions and behaviour patterns as a parent. See if you can spot yourself, and your mothering behaviour.

TYPE 1: The 'Always Happy' Mom
You seek or need approval:
- All that you do/all that your son does is being watched and judged.
- You have to please others to be liked.
- You want your son to approve of your decisions and to like you.
- Even when you are sad (or mad), you will smile.
- You often dismiss your own needs.

Your inner dialogue:
- *I am responsible for his happiness.*
- *His unhappiness makes me feel incompetent as a mother.*
- *Children should do what their mothers tell them. I am embarrassed if they don't. What would others think of them/me?*
- *A family must always be happy.*

TYPE 2: The 'I've Got This' Mom
You need to be in control:
- Deep down you fear being wrong or fear failure.
- You adopt a determined and organised approach to the world.
- Everything needs to go according to a plan.
- You believe that your plan is correct and justify this by moralising.
- You secretly dislike being questioned or criticised.

Your outer dialogue:
- *Do what I tell you.*
- *Because I say so.*
- *You're under my roof.*
- *Don't ever do that to me again!*
- *There is a right way and a wrong way.*
- *I know this stuff, so listen to me.*
- *It's for your own good.*

TYPE 3: The 'Cool' Mom
You need to be cool and appreciated (we all do!):
- You want your children to love you above all else.
- You place a premium on fun.
- You often dismiss serious subjects and often 'go with the flow'.
- You want to be around your children and want your teen son to want to be around you.
- You are prepared to go along with what your teen wants.

Your inner dialogue:
- *I'll give you everything I never had.*
- *I'll do whatever you want.*
- *I work/live for you. Let me make you happy.*
- *Life's about fun and we're buddies.*
- *Don't you and your friends think I'm cool?*

TYPE 4: The 'Fix-It' Mom
You need to sort stuff out:
- You are a 'do-gooder'; you will sort everything out for your family to make life easier.
- You believe a mother should take away any hassles or tough decisions from her children.
- You are a great doer and 'fixer'.
- You can be imposing through 'kindness'.

Your inner dialogue:
- *I have to make life easier for you.*
- *I can help by doing.*
- *I'll give you everything I've always wanted.*
- *I have to make everything right.*
- *I'm here for you whenever you want anything at all.*
- *I know what you need.*

TYPE 5: The 'Helpless' Mom
You feel incompetent:
- You may have been underparented yourself.
- You are unsure of yourself and can be ambivalent.

- You often feel anxious and are hesitant to set firm boundaries and stick to them.
- You are sensitive to criticism and can be reactive because of your feelings of inadequacy.
- You are often permissive for fear of conflict.
- You do what is expected.
- Depression can plague your parenting.

Your inner and outer dialogue:
- *Okay, where did I go wrong?*
- *What does his teacher/friend/Mr Smith say?*
- *I can't cope. I'm a mess.*
- *Children must please others and make others feel good.*
- *I must do what is 'right'.*
- *Help!*

TYPE 6: The 'Guilty' Mom

You feel you don't give enough:
- You may be very involved in your career and life outside the home.
- You feel that you do not have enough time or patience for your children.
- You do not feel available or competent, which often motivates you to overgive.
- There's usually some reason to feel that you have not created the right circumstances for your son.
- You are anxious about your parenting style.

Your inner dialogue:
- *My children's needs are more important than mine.*
- *I have to make up for not being there all the time.*
- *I need to make them happy all the time.*
- *My children can't like me. I'm always stressed.*
- *How can I make it up to him?*
- *I'm not good enough because I'm always exhausted.*
- *We don't do enough together.*

TYPE 7: The 'Resentful' or 'Competitive' Mom

You feel resentful and irritated:
- You are very self-focused and may be narcissistic.
- You think that children must just 'fit in'.
- You may not have really wanted to be a mother, or were idealistic about having children.
- You are often overtaxed by work or by your own personal or emotional life.
- You are an instant blamer.
- You can be rigid, with black-and-white thinking.

Your outer dialogue:
- *It's my children's fault that I am not …*
- *They take me for granted.*
- *Why do I always have to be the one?*
- *I'm drained of everything.*
- *I am responsible for everything and worth nothing.*
- *I never have enough time for myself.*
- *It is …'s fault.*
- *You get to have all the fun/fame/friends.*

TYPE 8: The 'Passive' Mom

You don't do structure:
- You don't follow a routine.
- You have low expectations.
- You use bribes to get results.
- You let the kids weigh in or ask for their input.
- You don't want to be the bad guy.
- You are stuck on repeat.
- You fear public outbursts.
- You have flexible rules.
- You avoid negative experiences.

Your inner dialogue:
- *I don't want to be seen as the 'bad guy'.*
- *I don't expect much.*
- *If I want results, I have to bribe my children to get them.*

- I'm unsure of myself, so I ask my children for their opinion.
- My children must respond positively every time.
- They can do what they want.

You may recognise yourself in a few of these moms. Human nature is complex and can change depending on your circumstances or your mood, so you may recognise yourself at different times in all these examples. Mothers often think that they can keep how they parent separate from how they are as human beings, but unfortunately all your wounds, triggers and negative belief systems will play out in your parenting. Your core beliefs about yourself are very relevant to how you parent.

For instance, the 'I've Got This' Mom will always react when her structure is disrupted or her children don't follow the rules. She can be 'put out' easily. On the other hand, the 'Helpless' Mom will react when she is questioned or challenged and will feel inadequate.

I also believe that we carry with us certain 'generation-specific' assumptions about children. They colour our decisions and communication. If these assumptions have not been reflected upon, they may also cause a rigid reaction.

RECOGNISE YOURSELF IN SPECIFIC NEEDS, FEARS OR BELIEF SYSTEMS

What can you do once you see yourself?
- Identify your assumptions: are they accurate or just old thinking habits?
- Identify your emotions when your son clashes with you.
- Check out your beliefs in the self-awareness questionnaire at the end of this chapter.
- Ask yourself: Are you operating with your values in mind?
- Identify your needs and fears, and how they affect your parenting.
- Be honest and become more flexible.
- Be more fluid, as it will help flow.

Who are you?
You are one of the most important figures, most important energies, in your son's life. You will continue to have a powerful influence on his life whether

you are in his presence or not. Make the decision right now that your influence is going to be one of beauty, grace, integrity, maturity and wisdom, because you have a powerful, wise woman within you. You are his mother!

For mothers of boys, it's very easy for us to think that we are just a back-up and a passenger who goes along for the ride, that we are only the support or the fan on the side lines. You are not – you are The Mother.

Don't get me wrong. Wise doesn't mean you can't lose it every now and then – that's life, that's real. Any boy that goes through life without hearing his mother shout and scream sometimes is going to quiver when his partner has a go at him! Your teen needs a mom who will sometimes throw down the gauntlet and speak up. But instead of leaving it for once a month when your oestrogen is a bit low, try to find within yourself the steady voice you can use to speak up about your own wants and needs, and the values that you believe in.

It's the same for moms of daughters. Reflect on the power of your own mother, whether you had her for many years or lost her when you were young. Even when our moms are not here, they influence us – sometimes, they influence us because we didn't like what they did, but they still influence us. The power your mother had over your life – whether it was good or bad – left an indelible mark. Mothers are powerful figures in our lives, psychologically and emotionally.

So, let's make a decision right now to come into our mothering and draw on all the shoulders we stand on – all the women who have gone before. Believe me, that energy is there – you just need to tap into it to find those values, and the way you want to be available in your home. You have learnt all the lessons you need to learn by the time you are in your forties. You've probably laid down all the rules that needed to be laid down in the family by now, and now you need to reflect on them and decide which are still important. We need to become a clear example of the type of person we would like our sons to be. In other words: be the change you want to see!

Post-divorce, I felt guilty, full of self-doubt, and a failure as a woman and a mother. I isolated myself, hiding from judgement, and feared I could lose custody of my precious boys. The universal energies must have pitied me, as I literally stumbled across a fierce 'earth' mother in the form of a therapist. She looked at me with eyes of compassion, yet with a backbone of iron and a formidable presence, and said, 'What are you doing? Dust yourself off, pick yourself up, and forget about what others think. You are a mother! You are the mother of those two boys. Have you any idea what that means? Being a mother comes with power. You just need to be open to it and welcome it!'

She then made me say out loud: 'I am your mother!' These words opened a cascade of energy. It was just waiting for me to invite myself in. I needed to consciously acknowledge the being within the mother role – the mother energy – which flows to any of us who has the precious grace to be a mom. This Great Mother energy also guides all women who open their hearts and choose to love and nurture themselves and others. It's fierce as fire. It's strong as rock. It's as gentle as a breeze and as wise as the earth. The Great Mother energy knows no bounds and is pure love. When you open yourself to its ancestral force and feel it, nothing can stop you from being what you need to be for your children. We can love and we can parent wisely. 'I am your mother!'

Your teen needs you to be a 'Wise and Empowered' Mom, one who is solidly within her own energy and comfortable with her own strength – a mom who is very clear about what she values, what she wants and what she doesn't want (based on personality, the home you run, the child you're dealing with, etc.). As my adult son tells me these days, 'Clear is kind. Unclear is unkind!', quoting a line from Brené Brown's book *Dare to Lead* (2018).

How to begin reflecting on yourself

Let's jump right in and contemplate our mothering habits in action:
- How do you talk to your son?
- What do you speak to him about?
- What types of conversations have you recently had?
- Did he start one?
- Did you?

Are these the typical things you say:
- *What did you eat?*
- *Did you go to extra maths?*
- *Did you apologise to your friend?*
- *How was school?*

Do you ask interrogative questions? And then leap in with a lecture when he doesn't respond?

We do this because we're trying to reach him. We're trying to start that conversation we're so desperate for. We turn into 'Interrogation' Moms. We don't want to, but we do. It's as if we've taken out a telescope and zoomed right in on him. We ask the same kinds of questions and get the same kinds of answers, over and over, and yet we still bring out that telescope:

1. When you notice that you're about to ask a habitual question, take a deep breath and just be. Be still but curious, present, open, loving and willing. See what happens. See what unfolds. On the journey deeper into this book, we're going to widen the telescope lens a little bit, so that we get to view the fullness of your son's life and personality. This is the first step: observing yourself and your habitual patterns, and then trying something different.
2. Write down your answers to these questions:
   - What are the emotions associated with being the mother of a teen boy?
   - What are the concerns, anxieties and questions that you have about being the mother of a teen boy?
   - How justified are these concerns?
   - How do you define your role as a mother?
   - Why are you reading this book?
   - What are the negative qualities you have experienced around men?
   - What are the positive masculine qualities that you have experienced?
3. Note what your expectations are of this book, and your intentions for now and the rest of your son's teen years.

REMEMBER: All energy moves towards the intentions we set. When you set down an intention that is really true to your heart, it will settle in your subconscious and guide the decisions you are making.

Explore your parenting style

The points below will help you to explore the areas that make up your parenting style. Read through them before tackling the worksheet at the end of this chapter.

1. Your history and how you were parented.
The best predictor of how you will parent is how you were parented. How did you experience your parents, and how did that affect you then and now? Are you repeating some ineffective parenting skills? What were their shoulds and shouldn'ts? How did you get their attention – by compliance or defiance? Try to remember your reactions. There is also the generational difference that comes into play. Our '60s-generation parents (influenced by the war) were obsessed with 'Waste not, want not' and 'If it's not bleeding, you're fine!' The '80s-generation parents were focused on 'Don't squash a child's spirit', whereas the millennial parents are obsessed with science-based research on parenting or 'If you want to know it, google it.'

2. Where are you in your life right now?
What is your context? Are you satisfied with where you are now? How do you feel about your work life, social life, relationships? How balanced or stressed are you? Are there areas that need to be worked on and developed further? Understand the phase of life you are in now. If you are in your forties or fifties, it is a time of questioning and reassessing. It is also a time of hormonal adjustments that will impact how you look and feel. It is a time of being more discerning and gaining confidence as a woman to do more of what you want and need. If you are dissatisfied or have regrets, this will affect your mothering. Often, small, practical adjustments can make a huge difference. Write a list of your goals on all levels, think about your values and what you would like to achieve in life, and write a mission statement for yourself.

3. Know your emotions.
Teens will push your emotional buttons, and you need to know when and why you react. Knowing your hopes and fears allows you to understand your trigger points. We all have deep emotional scars, and being aware of them helps us become less defensive. If you become comfortable with exposing your vulnerabilities to your teens and partner, you become a role model when raising emotionally intelligent men. Hormonal changes will also impact on your emotional life, so knowing your emotions and learning how to self-regulate will help you sort out distress honestly and assertively. Stating your real needs and wants will clear the air and help everyone feel connected to an authentic person who has authority over her own life.

4. Know your strengths and weaknesses as a human being.
Do this without judgement or criticism of yourself. You will need your unique strengths to raise a son. Know your core beliefs, the good and the bad, because this often sets the tone for what you expect of yourself and others. Empowerment is about accepting and being who you really are, verbalising it, and creating clear boundaries about what we will or won't accept as women. Without even knowing it, we have created 'false' personas to please others. It's time to drop the masks. If you find yourself saying 'What if …' or 'You should …', then you can be guaranteed that you are more worried about what others think than your own son's well-being. We all have weaknesses and vulnerabilities, and sometimes a horrid ego that is obsessed with being perfect. Embrace the concept of *wabi-sabi* – the Japanese principle of accepting imperfection as a way of life. Celebrate who you are *now* and what *is*, as opposed to how you should be.

IDENTIFY YOUR CORE BELIEFS

Our lives often revolve around a few (often cultural) core beliefs. They can motivate or deflate us. Not being 'enough' of something is a very common cultural belief, mostly as a result of endless comparisons via social media. A core belief is always an 'I' statement, as in *I am unlovable*. Some common core beliefs are:

- *I am not good enough.* (incompetent)
- *I am not smart enough.* (stupid)
- *I am not pretty enough.* (ugly)
- *I will not be loved by anyone.* (unlovable)
- *I am unwanted.* (bad)
- *I am too different.* (odd)
- *I am always wrong.* (unacceptable)

A negative core belief affects others' reactions, and you then believe it is true, so it becomes a self-fulfilling prophecy. This leads us to really believe we are flawed and unworthy, and 'evidence' begins to confirm this. It's a vicious circle of reinforcement.

How to challenge your core beliefs
Next time you are faced with a difficult situation that causes you anxiety or feelings of depression, think about your instinctive first thoughts – your automatic thought about yourself AND the situation – and then try to identify the underlying core belief. Here are some common core beliefs about life:
- *Life isn't fair.*
- *People are basically good/bad.*
- *The world is a dangerous place.*

Once you've identified your personal and circumstantial core beliefs, try to challenge them by asking yourself if they are always true, or if there could be times when they are not true. This process could lead you to a more reasonable outlook on life, improving your self-esteem and emotions.

Core beliefs and reality
Our core beliefs create our reality by filtering what we perceive as true or real. For each of us, the world we live in exists only in our minds. The narratives we tell ourselves impact the decisions we make. Teens should be told that they can misjudge something in the heat of the moment. For some mothers, your teen smoking pot is proof of your failure as a mother; for others, it's proof of a normal teen.

Alternative ways to frame your reality
We can change our core beliefs over time by reframing our reality. Ask yourself:

Are my thoughts in tune with objective reality?
Can I be guaranteed that what I think will happen will definitely happen?
Does this always happen or have there been some exceptions in my life?

Choose to think more optimistic thoughts and explore alternative assumptions. Take a different perspective and imagine an ideal outcome. How does the ideal outcome affect your feelings and register in your body? This sets up what you choose to attract in the future.

The best phase of my life journey started when I began to be anchored in my authentic core – that core that lies beyond all the concepts about who I am. And once I had faced my negative core beliefs and began to accept the good, the bad and the mediocre within, a core of calm began to make itself at home. This has helped me to remain authentic and centred (the majority of the time) no matter what my sons throw at me or what life presents.

Have you noticed the negative core beliefs within?
Can you name the obvious ones?
Can you commit to reframing destructive thoughts?
Is it possible to begin to accept and love yourself?

HOW CONSCIOUS ARE YOU OF YOUR PARENTING STYLE?

When looking at the diagram below, bear in mind that eventually we want our parenting style to move to include positive permissiveness and be more democratic.

'Permissiveness' has a negative side, yet your parenting does need to lead to a place where you are handing over a lot more, especially towards the end of your son's school career. This I call positive permissiveness.

In contrast, the top-down, authoritarian approach of 'my way or the highway' leads to low independence, low self-esteem, and either a passive or a rigid child. And if we are inappropriately permissive at the wrong age and let them do what they want, when they want, how they want ... then obviously we are going to see poor self-control and immature development.

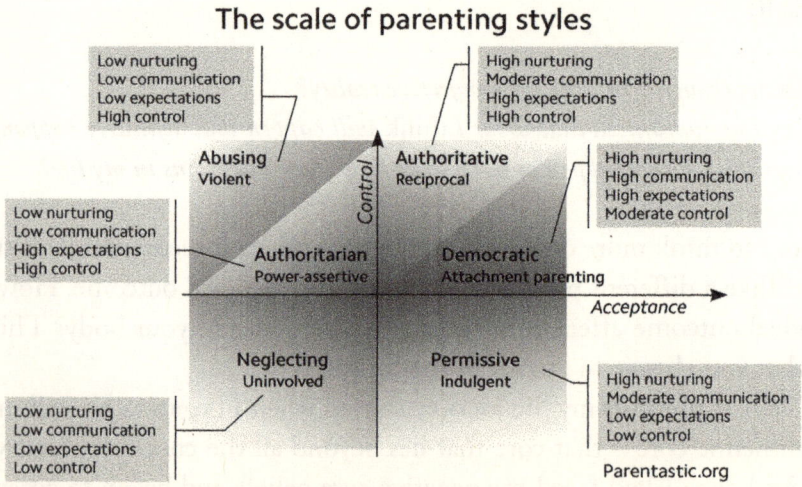

(*Source*: Adapted from Maccoby and Martin, 1983)

The top right-hand side of the diagram – authoritative and democratic – shows the ideal balance, where you make the rules, but also have discussions, debates and dialogue. You are allowing your son to make his own decisions more and more. And once he has made a decision and it turns out to be a mistake, you don't overreact, but instead use the opportunity to discuss what was learnt from the situation in a conversation grounded in growth:

What can be done differently so that next time I can practise trusting again?
What is it that you are going to do when you go to someone else's house?

It's still a constant process of being firm but fair, and understanding at which developmental level he is, until he moves into being a boy who is able to be self-reliant, self-controlled, self-disciplined, self-motivated and more flexible in his capacities.

This is the growth mindset, but it is not letting go of your parenting values, or your parenting needs and style.

> **Worksheet: Homework**
> **Determine your parenting style**
> Choose one of the following responses for each of the scenarios in the table below:
> **A:** *I decide; I may discuss it, yet I expect my son to do as I say.*
> **B:** *I discuss it, I practise compromise, but I usually make the final decision.*
> **C:** *I let my son make his own decisions.*

How would you approach the following issues?	A	B	C
Buying or wearing of bizarre clothes that he wears out of school			
Wanting an unconventional hairstyle during the holidays			
Music or TV playing while doing homework			
Wanting to drop a school subject			
Wanting to give up a musical instrument			
Going to pop concerts with friends before age 15			
Dating at age 13			
Smoking			
Having a house party at age 16 because you won't be there			
Wanting to sleep over at a friend's house after a party			
Deciding what time to come home from a party			
Wanting to drink alcohol at age 16			
Wanting to go out on a school night			
Not wanting to tell you where he is going with his friends			
Deciding how he wants to spend his pocket money			
Deciding on a career after school			
Wanting to take on a part-time holiday job			
Deciding how much he helps in the house			
Not wanting to go along to a family outing			
Hanging out with a friend who you think is taking drugs			
Wanting to decorate his room himself			
Cleaning his untidy room			
Deciding how much or how little he eats, and what he eats			

More As: Authoritarian style
Here the parents make all the decisions. Children must obey and 'do as I say'. Parents are the head of the house and their children must fit in. This approach limits self-expression and offers conditional affirmation, often resulting in the teen showing a 'false self' to please the parent. Good self-esteem and development of autonomy are delayed.

Mainly Bs: Authoritative style
This is a firm but fair approach. It is a negotiating parenting style. Children are clear on boundaries, and communication channels are always kept open. The child feels important to parents and household decisions. It promotes decision-making skills and allows informed independence. The child learns that there are consequences for any of his decisions that break rules. Relationships with responsibility become all-important.

Mainly Cs: Negatively permissive style
Here the parents are unsure of and unclear about boundaries and rules. Structure is not available and the child is given too much power. Parents are often too busy or caught up in their own lives to really be in touch with what the child needs. The child does things his own way, although he lacks the skills and foresight. He may grow up with a sense of entitlement or restlessness.

Note: Cs may increase if you have a responsible son or he is older than eighteen.

> **Ask Megan**
>
> **Question:** '*I feel I am not fun any more. Most of my conversations with my son involve me trying to show him a better way, or sort him out.*'
>
> **Answer:** '*It's easy to slip into this role as a parent. It's the moraliser in you or the fix-it mom! You need to challenge and change this for yourself.*' See Chapter 4 and practise being 'Coach' Mom.

Are you operating from a fear-based parenting style?

When your son tells you a story, what is the attention you bring to him? Is it:

What's wrong here?
What's the problem?
What's the concern here?
What needs to be sorted out here?

We spend a lot of time in judgement mode or trying to take over control. This doesn't work with teenagers who are trying to find their own way and their own solutions.

The good news is that there is another way of being, and it is as simple as looking for what's right in the moment, what's enjoyable, and what we can actually learn in the moment.

You can go with a 'judgement mentality', where you are always looking for problems, or you can choose a 'growth mentality', where you suspend the voice of judgement and try to adjust to the question: What is there to learn?

What is right in the moment when your teen boy is telling you a story is that he has brought his attention to you. When you look at it like that, you're going think again about the quality of attention you give him.

An attitude of judgement stops us from approaching an interaction with an open mind. What suspends and arrests the open heart? The voice of cynicism or suspicion. The voice that says:

You expect me to believe that?
I don't trust this.
This doesn't feel right.
Something is going on here.

You are used to making things right, fixing your little boy's problems, healing his hurts, protecting him … It has become your default position. You are primed to look out for anything wrong, and that's immediately the place your mind jumps to. Mistrust causes a sudden contraction and, when you're closed and suspicious, you can't be available in an open, heartfelt way.

Fear sabotages your willingness to be present. You need to begin to find a way to be more loving than fearful, because you are laying down a legacy in your home of being worried all the time. You probably parent in an unconscious way if you are often anxious.

Instead, you want to project fearlessness:

You can do it!
I trust you.
Let's have some fun!

What, then, can help us move into being more willing, more available and more open? How can we find ways to lessen our fearfulness as a parent?

That is what I hope this book will show you. One of the major things we will be doing is discovering that the more you parent from a place of fear, the more you are establishing an ancient system of submission and domination. That system is caused by high stress.

The more you are in high stress, the closer you are to fight-or-flight mode, which results in a state of submission and domination:

I have to be right, and therefore you have to be wrong.
I have to be in charge, and therefore you have to follow.
I will tell you what to do and you better just listen up.

This causes a downward spiral of blame and shame. Instead, choose a cooperative and relational approach by practising having an open heart, an open mind, and a willingness to be brave and vulnerable enough to be receptive and available. You will learn to move into a place of cooperation, contribution, sharing, caring, loving, being more open and being more available.

Can you do it 100 per cent of the time? No, but you are going to work towards establishing pockets of that in your home – moments that will begin to diminish the stress that keeps you so trapped in the belief that life is tough and hard. We want our teenagers to have some hope that life can be joyful and fun, that they can be liked and that they can follow their bliss, and discover the things that are important to them.

> ### Worksheet: Re-parenting the self
> Approach with curiosity and a tender touch. Give the self-critic some time off:
> - In what ways did your mother help you as a child?
> - What do you imagine you needed from her the most as a teen?
> - Does this impact on how you mother now? How?
> - Can you understand how this affected your emotional growth?
> - Have you wondered how your son would describe you? How?
>
> Reflect on your behaviour in relationships as a result of your upbringing. By looking at your own life and how you were raised, you can get a more expansive view of your mothering approach.
>
> Rate your self-esteem at the moment:
> 0 = *I loathe myself.*   10 = *I love and accept everything about myself.*
>
> Rate how content you are with your life:
> 0 = *I hate my situation.*   10 = *I am fully satisfied with and enjoy my life situation.*
>
> - What dreams, desires and hopes for yourself have you not achieved?
> - What are the personal or situational obstacles preventing you from achieving what you desire for yourself?
> - Does this in any way influence how you raise your son?
> - Do you over- or underemphasise certain of his personality traits or goals?

> ### Worksheet: Homework
> Make a list of your WANTS (physical or doable things) and your NEEDS (internal satisfiers, emotions or character strengths):
> - My WANTS: _____
>   _____
>   My NEEDS: _____
>   _____

What needs do your wants highlight? (For example, security, recognition, status, attention, affection, respect, happiness, purpose, to belong, fun, approval, acceptance, fame, to be in control, appreciation.)
- What do you worry about the most?
- Is this related to your needs?
- What is your main worry for your family/your son?
- Does this relate in any way to your own upbringing or your parents' worries?
- Are these worries in tune with reality?

When our fears are triggered, we react. (For example, anger, denial, panic, anxiety, withdrawal, disappointment.)
- What are your typical negative reactions towards your son?
- What are the general things that you normally react negatively to with your son?
- When he behaves like that, what are your spontaneous responses?

Is there a possibility that your son is reflecting your own fears and reactions, or are you misjudging his mood because of your own state of being?

> **REMEMBER:** You and your teen will not always act as expected. Your mood or anxiety can intervene in the moment. Talking things through *before* the event and staying calm will help.

CHAPTER 2

How to have better parenting conversations

'Great minds discuss ideas; average minds discuss events; small minds discuss people.'

– Eleanor Roosevelt

'I'm not coming to the family lunch you've organised this weekend. I'm going to stay with a friend.'

Bam! Red flag.

You feel attacked. Annoyed. Challenged. Angry.

You are about to react and make some fundamental parenting errors.

Now, we all know that to a greater or lesser degree males are competitive. So, when we take the conversation to a place where it's a direct attack on the boy in front of you, what's the outcome going to be?

He's either going to fight back, or he's going to withdraw.

It is always much better to move towards two-way dialogue. We know this in our hearts. So why is it that some of us tend to be reactive? Why do we fall into these patterns of communication when they clearly don't work? What is that about? Is it stress? Time pressure? Hormones? Or is your short fuse just part of your personality?

If we're stuck in this pattern where we only react to people in a heightened way, it means that we might be holding on to some old but very strict beliefs about ourselves:

I'm the most important person in the room.
I don't need to listen to anybody else.
What I say is right.

But it can also come from a place of hurt:

Why isn't anyone listening to me?
No one takes me seriously.
I'm always last in the queue.

One day, I noticed a pattern of mine and it sounded like this: 'But you are not listening to me!' I said it about twenty times before I realised that I was not only saying it to my son again and again, but also in my love relationship. BINGO! A pattern was emerging from a wounded place of not being heard. To overcome this pattern, I had to explore early childhood pain of not being encouraged to voice my feelings. I had to practise self-care to allow me to discover a more secure response.

Being very reactive in intense situations can mean that we are stuck in a place where we believe we are not heard or not listened to with the respect we deserve, or that we think we're not approved of, or that we're unappreciated. Such beliefs mean that we will react in a certain way when that emotion is triggered. It can be a hangover from a time long ago when you were hurt and you held these beliefs about yourself – the behaviour has become a habit, even though you may have healed the pain from the past.

If we find that our default response is a heightened reaction, we have to train ourselves to be able to drop out of this reactive position for any parenting to be effective. We have to say, 'Right, time to move into more of a listening mode, to self-regulate, to calm my response to the stress, panic or anxiety that this situation is triggering.'

LAWS OF COMMUNICATING WITH A TEEN BOY

In Chapter 4, I am going to give you the seven steps to tackle any parenting problem. But for now, let's unpack and understand what you are doing wrong:
- Spend more time with him.
- Turn off the screen or put your phone or book down.
- Avoid texting when your son is talking to you.
- Unless other people are specifically meant to be included, hold conversations in private.
- Don't embarrass him in front of others.

- If you are very angry, don't attempt communication until you regain your cool.
- Don't interrupt when he is trying to tell his story.
- Avoid correcting him unless it is absolutely necessary.
- Try to listen and ask questions, not lecture.
- Don't ask 'why'. Ask 'what' happened.
- Show that you accept him, regardless of what he has or has not done.
- Affirm his efforts to communicate.
- Give him time and space.
- Don't expect too much, or lower your high expectations.

Staying connected
Try to do the following:
- Listen.
- Mirror and share.
- Encourage and validate.
- Be open and empathise.
- Spend unplugged time with him.
- Do stuff together.

Avoid the following:
- Criticising.
- Blaming.
- Shaming.

Avoid saying the following:
- *You can talk when I'm finished.*
- *Don't talk to me like that.*
- *I know what's best for you.*
- *Just do what I say and that will solve the problem.*
- *You shouldn't feel that way.*
- *Don't say that.*
- *That is just stupid.*
- *Don't be dumb.*

The most important thing in communicating is that you have to listen and attune to him.

At the heart of my parenting philosophy is my belief in building relationships.

I encourage you to keep trying to move to a place where, instead of rules and facts and getting things done, you are always building a relationship with your son. It may mean you forget that he left his socks on the floor when there is relationship tension.

> '*Out beyond the ideas of wrongdoing and rightdoing, there is a field. I'll meet you there ...*'
> – **Rumi**

Rumi sums it up beautifully. This field is a place of no labels or judgements, but of trying to understand and be with each other.

But this seldom happens. Instead of connecting, you are 'sorting stuff out'. This is a doing approach and not a 'being together' one.

Yes, you will always have to do the chores, and problem-solve, and work, and mother. You will always be busy, but time goes by so fast and, by the time he finishes school, you are going to think, 'Who is this boy? I actually don't know what his favourite colour is. I don't know what his favourite movies are. I've never played a computer game with him. We don't even have a hobby together. We don't have a relationship.'

By then it's almost too late, because the moment he leaves your home, the opportunities that you have right now are gone.

But what do you prioritise? Getting things done? Sorting things out? Or having a real home that protects the hearts and minds of the people in it? How do we create this sanctuary for our family for broadening minds, opening hearts and making room for differences?

There is a way – there absolutely is a way.

Moving away from controlling and judging

In parenting, we tend to exercise control and impose judgement, which could lead you to criticise without even meaning to. You might hear the following words come out of your mouth:

> *Why on earth did you do that?*
> *What an odd thing to do!*
> *What a mean thing to say!*
> *Where's this mean streak in you coming from?*

You find yourself falling into this manner of conversation in a tense situation, where you might assassinate his character. Human nature is such that the more fearful we are, the more we try to control or attack.

As women, we intuitively pick up on a mood in our home. How many of us have said the following to our boys?:

Your bad moods are affecting all of us.
Can't you wipe that sulky look off your face?
I can't eat supper looking at your glum face.

So, we are aware that his internal mood can affect the environment, but what we are less aware of is that our own inner state affects our parenting.

One of the important things to acknowledge when it comes to parenting, and particularly conscious parenting, is that we have different levels of communication in our conversations. Our level of communication differs from person to person. Think about those times in your life when you were able to have a deep, meaningful conversation – you felt comfortable and were able to share quite a lot of your personal feelings, and the person you were talking to shared theirs. What allows this to happen?

There is a kind of synchronicity that is going on where you feel comfortable with each other – maybe you share similar values, backgrounds or belief systems – so it's easier to have a deeper conversation. But it's not only about what is said. It's how you are listened to and how you listen to the other person. I think one of the major factors that allow for a deeper, more comfortable conversation is that neither party feels that they are being judged by the other. The moment you start feeling judged or criticised, you are either going to shut down or become argumentative or defensive.

And here's the kicker: the best way to influence an outcome is by your energetic presence. Call it your attitude, if you want. I like to call it presence. The more centred, open and available you are to the present moment, the more positively you influence the 'field' – the space between us, and the space that surrounds all living beings. It's also the energy field that we sense in nature – it has its own mysterious intelligence. Christianity calls it the Holy Spirit. Many modern spiritual leaders refer to it as the evolutionary impulse that guides all of life. Carl Jung calls it the collective unconscious that influences us. Jung said that humans need to believe in something 'bigger' than themselves. I always tell the parents of teens that if they once believed in God, angels or spiritual intelligence, now is the time to reignite that belief. It really helps if your son has his own soul journey, and is guided by a sacred intelligence.

Being the adult in the room

When people fly off the handle and react emotionally, it is a sign of some form of emotional immaturity.

Emotional maturity requires an ability to identify your emotions and to regulate them: you feel the emotion, but take a moment to pause and be sensible. As emotionally mature adults, we should be able to control our emotions and reactions.

The first thing you need to do is **regulate your emotions** – and this is a skill your son also needs to learn. It is really important that he learns to calm himself when his emotions are triggered. You actually know the techniques. When we were your son's age, our grannies told us to count to ten, take a deep breath, step away for a moment … We know what technique works, but we don't apply it any more. Think of what your intention is here: even though you want a good relationship with your son, you also want to get your point across. You want your son to listen to you with attention and respect … Isn't that what he wants from you, too? If you're both shouting at each other, no one is listening, no one is showing respect and no one is getting their point across.

So, try this instead. When a situation arises and you feel yourself reacting emotionally, say to yourself, 'This is not about me. Let me just widen my view and change my perspective. I'm going to pause, breathe, and try to see this from my son's point of view for a moment.' And then I will paraphrase what he says, followed by a calmly asked question, and then I will listen, and listen …

Remember, your son will mirror the environment around him. So, if you give a heightened reaction to his statement, you're going to get a heightened reaction right back. If you project calm, he's more likely to reflect calm back. You can then get to the bottom of the issue and tell him how you feel, and you can learn how he feels, and why. You've skipped the confrontation and moved to intentional dialogue. Great! But, just as important, you're also teaching him the correct response in this type of situation.

So, the first step you take to avoid reaction mode is to consciously lower the anxiety within yourself and step into a more responsive space.

There are some techniques that will help you get to a calm place, where your observation is curious, non-judgemental and very present.

If you feel your anxiety or stress levels rise when he challenges you, visualise breathing down into the earth (out), and back up into your belly. Feel yourself solidly, feet on the floor, there and present. Try to clear your mind and, no matter what he says or how he says it, soften your heart.

But what's the one sure way you can do that? Think of him at age five, six or seven, on his first day of school, or fast asleep on your lap or in your arms – just hold that picture in your mind and you'll find that your heart will completely soften all over again. And you need a soft heart to move from reaction to responsive, from ping-pong opinion debates to empathic listening and empathic communication, understanding and dialogue. It can take time for both of you, but eventually you will both get there. I can guarantee it.

When we participate in a heart-to-heart conversation, we are more open-minded – open to listening and receiving the information that is being shared. You're being more open-hearted because you've softened yourself, and made yourself available and are present in the situation. And you've dropped your own agenda because you're coming with a willingness and an intention to be curious.

What shuts down an open heart, open mind and open will? Criticism, disappointment, cynicism, disbelief, lack of trust, judgement ... When you have any of these at the forefront of your mind, it's going to be really hard to hear what your son has to say without jumping to conclusions or judgements or criticisms, all of which are sure-fire ways of shooting down a conversation before it can start.

The moment you are able, move into curiosity and say to yourself, 'Let me try to be more open-minded.' You will feel the safe space that you're creating for the conversation, which will result in more interconnectedness, and invite opportunities for a heart-to-heart conversation. The entire atmosphere will become more supportive of your good intentions. If this is a challenge for you, imagine the best possible outcome and incubate the feelings that give rise to this.

Challenge: Change your habitual language

Mindfulness can mean widening your perspective to take in the whole context. A more expansive approach to dealing with a teen issue or a family impasse is to change perspective and to broaden your view. Or to simply find a more enjoyable or tongue-in-cheek way of saying something. Not everything about raising teens needs to be serious.

Finding the humour is essential, because it will stop your teen in his tracks. I have found a fun and easy way to do this by reframing questions/statements:

Instead of: *What's the problem here?*
Try saying: *What can you learn from this challenge?*

Instead of: *Stop this immediately!*
Try saying: *Why are you finding this so enticing?*

Instead of: *Your behaviour is making me mad!*
Try saying: *I notice you are trying a different way to do this.*

Instead of: *You are shouting!*
Try saying: *I notice you are playing with volume today.*

Instead of: *That is so stupid.*
Try saying: *I see you are experimenting with an interesting approach to this.*

Instead of: *You are rude!*
Try saying: *Does this approach feel good to you?*

Instead of: *This is so selfish.*
Try saying: *Is this a way of you claiming your autonomy?*

Instead of: *You are so ungrateful.*
Try saying: *I suggest you are not seeing the bigger picture right now.*

Instead of: *You are lazy.*
Try saying: *I notice this does not ignite or inspire you.*

Instead of: *Your room is untidy.*
Try saying: *Well, this is a creative arrangement of your belongings.*

Instead of: *Stop fighting!*
Try saying: *I notice you feel strongly/passionately about …*

> Instead of: *That's obnoxious.*
> Try saying: *You have an interesting opinion.*

What if he is downright rude?

Sometimes, your son's agenda will prevent a dialogue from occurring. Sometimes, he will be downright rude. I am not suggesting that you accept that. But it doesn't mean that you should slip back into reaction mode either. Calm yourself down, bring your curiosity and, instead of criticising, ask, 'How do you feel about what you just did? Do you feel proud of yourself right now?'

Remember, we're not saying this in a sarcastic or critical way – we're simply curious: 'Is this something you admire about yourself? What would make you feel good right now? What would you do in this situation to help you feel good about yourself?' Simple. You're giving responsibility back to him, so that he makes his own reference around what a fine young man really is. It's how you ask the question that is important: with genuine curiosity, not knowing the answer in your head. See what comes from him. Most times he won't be able to answer, so what is the next thing you say? 'You know what, why don't you take some time and think about it? I'm not going to give you the answer, because my answer is not your answer.' You hand it over, and that makes him feel more empowered.

And he *will* think about it. One thing I can tell you about your son is that when you ask him to think about something, I promise you that he does. You may never hear back, or it might come out a month or a year later, but he will think about it. We have to stop trying to provide the answers and let him come to them himself.

What if every conversation is a debate?

Sometimes, every conversation seems to turn into a debate – his opinion against yours. We need to work out how we can start moving from debating and reacting to responding and dialoguing. You may not be able to do it when he's thirteen or fourteen, but begin to focus on the direction you want to go in. At sixteen, there is massive brain development, which continues into your son's twenties, so from age sixteen you will find that there is suddenly an opportunity for deep dialogue. I refer to this level of conversation as Level 4 (see page 43).

LEVELS OF CONNECTION

An essential ingredient of conscious parenting is the capacity to listen deeply – to others, and to what our true nature calls us to do. Through active and open listening, we deepen our relationships and become mindful communicators. It is the quality of attention that is the magic ingredient of good connection and heartfelt communication.

Some years back, I attended a workshop based on Otto Scharmer's seminal facilitation approach called Theory U. I found his idea of different levels of listening (habitual, factual, empathic, generative) very useful for parenting. I've added in another level because, after years of working as a psychotherapist, I found conversing and connecting to another does not just jump from empathic connection to generative connection.

Connection levels	Emotional maturity	Conversing	Brain
1. Habitual, unconscious	Stuck Closed Blame Victim mentality	Downloading Unaware Controlling Finger-pointing Dismissive	Level 1: Brain stem
2. Factual, black or white	Ego Self-centred Fight or flight Not trusting	Debate Competitive *Do*-ing	Level 2: Hindbrain (survival)
3. Empathic, honest, flexible	Self-responsibility Heartfelt Self-awareness	Negotiate Ask Goal-directed	Level 3: Midbrain (limbic)
4. Aligned mentally, emotionally, physically	Coherent Authentic Open Committed	Natural dialogue Relaxed exchange Real Growth essential	Level 4: Left and right brain (coherence)
5. Generative, discerning, listening inwards and outwards equally	Unitive Community aware Higher service In flow Head, heart and field Cosmic consciousness	Inspiring Collective Creative Expressive Quiet Process-orientated *Be*-ing	Level 5: Pineal (prefrontal cortex)

(*Source*: Adapted from Otto Scharmer, *Theory U: Leading from the future as it emerges*, 2009)

LEVEL 1: Information and instruction

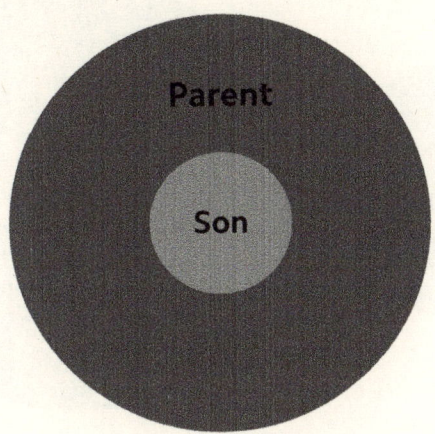

Unconscious parenting

At Level 1, you are listening from your habits, from what you already know. The result is that you reconfirm what you already knew:

My way is right and you must listen to it.

Conversation at Level 1 (for example, 'Brush your teeth', 'Go to bed', 'Take the dirty washing out of the laundry bin') has its place, but if your awareness is at this level, it's a fairly unconscious form of conversing, because you put yourself or the parenting position first. The child is totally absorbed by what the parent wants, how they want it done and when they want it done:

- You are confirming what you know; the past is very relevant. You parent as you were parented – without insight. Expectations rule.
- You are focused on problems – telescope parenting.
- You say what the other wants to hear. You are possibly polite or pleasing – insecure position.
- You are controlling and reacting (from the reptilian brain) – authoritarian.
- You see parenting as a role to be performed 'right'.
- You have a right and wrong mentality – unconscious parenting.

Being in survival mode blocks any flow. Ask yourself: *When do I operate like this?*

LEVEL 2: Facts are shared

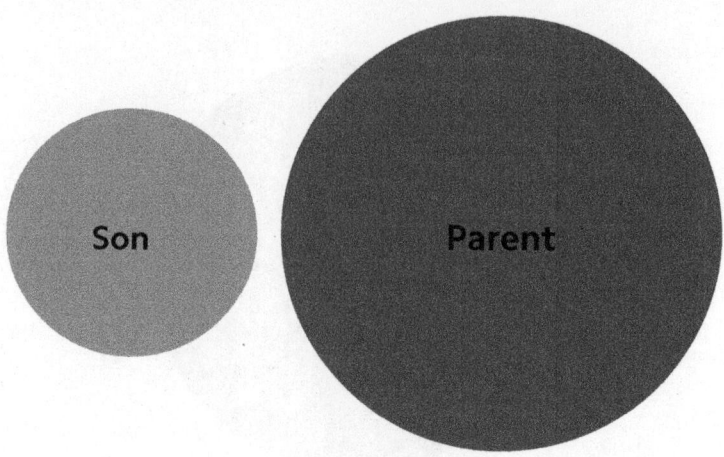

Parallel parenting

At Level 2, you are noticing something new, something that differs from what you already knew or expected to hear:

I heard something new that's different from my opinion, BUT ... I am the parent and you are the child, and you must listen to my advice.

In conversation at Level 2, we move into a phase where facts are shared. So, you discuss things with your son, and he begins to have more of a say. When facts are shared, there is an opportunity to learn something new: you listen, but most of the time you are more involved in stating your view. Your son is talking to you and expressing his opinions, but you already have your answers in your head, and you really want to launch back with, 'Did you think of the consequences of that?' It is a 'Yes ... BUT ...' scenario. As parents, our conversation is normally at Level 2:

*Okay, I'll listen to what you are saying, but we are doing what I'm saying.
I'll listen, yes, I'll take the time, yes, but I'm not changing my mind.*

We are still at a factual level. There's no self-reflection, self-censorship or self-auditing happening – we're reacting in the moment. It's usually a habitual way of being: you rush into the situation with the same approach each time. Level 2 is basically about just looking for facts and information:

- You state your view/case. You are opinionated: 'I will sort this out!'
- You have a competitive edge when some of your viewpoints are challenged.
- You allow another to talk and new data is heard, yet you stick to your facts.
- You keep the peace by holding back deeper views or are fearful of venturing into new feelings.
- You believe roles still operate in opposing ways (for example, mother versus son).
- You will begin to initiate a shared listening, but will be quick to show where your son is wrong and the consequences of his behaviour.
- You are mostly interested in your son hearing your point of view.
- You hope to change his behaviour via imparting information.
- Right/wrong is still important and you use a reward system only.

At this level, it becomes fact versus fact, opinion versus opinion, barter versus barter. There is a place for this up to and into the teens. But once your son turns thirteen, Level 3 should be the goal that you want to achieve. Only an open mind and an open heart will lead you to the next level.

Ask yourself: *When is this kind of listening appropriate?*

LEVEL 3: Heart is open and feelings matter

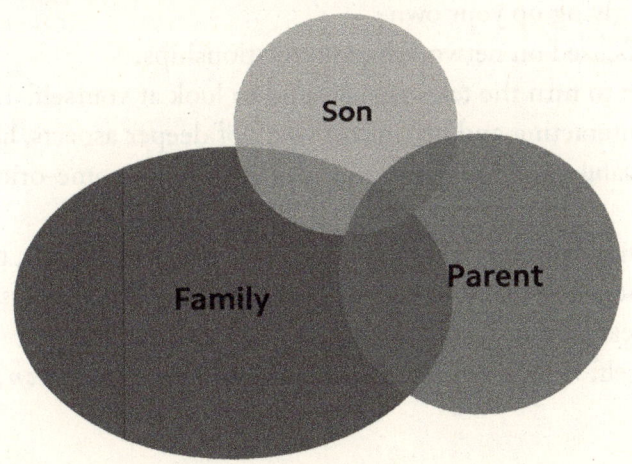

Relational parenting

At Level 3, you are listening empathically and experiencing/sensing an emotional connection:

I have a point of view AND so do you.
We influence each other sometimes.
I'm hoping we can embrace your way of doing things.

In conversation at Level 3, we open ourselves up and try to listen to the other person; we place a priority on understanding. We love this boy who is growing into his own unique character, and we feel empathic towards his thoughts and opinions.

At Level 3, you will be engaging in open-hearted conversing. You begin to feel that deeper emotions lie below the surface. You become aware of meaningful aspects such as values and life quests, yet you still remain goal- or outcome-orientated. Your son can't yet say, 'I'm feeling rejected by my friend because he went off with another guy at break,' but you know that there's a feeling churning inside him.

As a parent, you begin to encourage a 'growth mindset' by helping him to understand that every struggle he encounters enables a deeper viewpoint and more empathy, and develops our inner resources:

- You see through your son's eyes and make space for him.
- You are interested in your son's growth and development.
- You are open to understanding and appreciating his perspective, and even giving up your own.
- You are focused on networking and relationships.
- You begin to turn the telescope around to look at yourself.
- You are interacting and becoming aware of deeper aspects, like feelings, values and life quests, but you are still outcome-orientated.

You are moving towards what's good for you and your family, towards the parent as coach. You demonstrate reflection and investigate possible lessons both of you can learn.

Ask yourself: *What conditions are necessary for me to converse on this level?*

LEVEL 4: Coherent and aligned

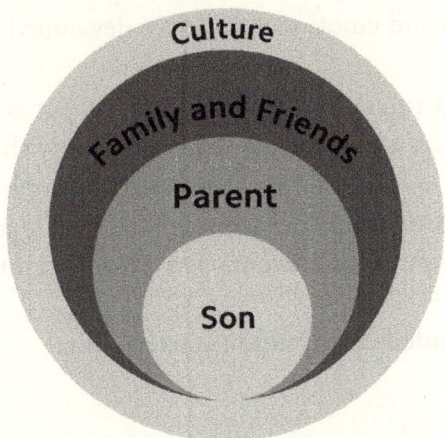

Coherent and aligned parenting

At Level 4, you are attuned to your son's inner essence. You sense his separate life force yearning to express itself. You are curious about his potential. You strive to be authentic.

> *I am curious to know all of you and be attuned to your expression ... I hope we can both be open, authentic and converse about meaningful things.*

You listen deeply, with your whole being, because you are interested. You understand that he does not have all the social and emotional skills to fully express himself. You are more focused on your own communication and presence, knowing that you are a role model. Conversation is much more organic and flows from facts to negotiations, to questions, to sharing, to listening, to empathising. You discuss events, happenings, news and ideas.

- You are open to his ideas about a wide range of topics.
- You are curious about your son and encourage his voice and feelings.
- You are focused on solutions and positive-speak.
- You listen with your whole body and being.
- You make room for intuition and sensing and natural flow.
- You pause, take time out and focus on your energy.
- Your open mind, open heart and open conversation help you to attune to where your son is at.

- You see yourself as coach, yet realise that your authenticity is essential.
- You understand that his growth and development are important.
- Your relationship and emotional skills are developed.

You are now aligned to your son's inner essence, yet authentic enough to share your true feelings and ideas too. You converse with much more clarity and confidence and do not feel threatened when his opinion opposes yours. You always see his potential and encourage his best ideas. It's *real* conversation now, where you discuss events as well as personal reflections and philosophical topics.

Try some open-ended conversation starters, like:
- *How was it ...?*
- *In what ways ...?*
- *I'd love you to tell me about ...*
- *What's it like ... I'm curious ...?*
- *What if ...?*
- *I'd love your opinion about ...*

LEVEL 5: Will and intention are both open

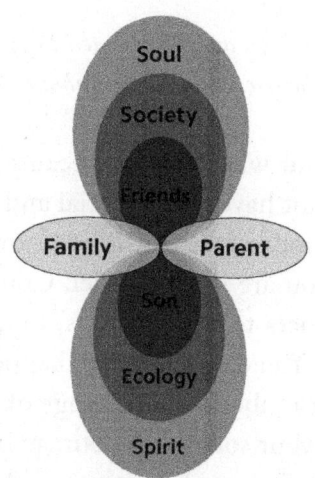

Dynamic and interconnected parenting

At Level 5, you are connecting to the emerging future – a future possibility that connects to your and your son's emerging self, to where you both feel authentic and creative:

I sincerely care and include your full well-being.
We are all on a journey together and open to discovering a new way.

We have all had conversations at Level 5. It's when you meet a friend, a like-minded soul, or a person who shares a common mental challenge, and you have a real conversation. You get into the nitty-gritty of things through sharing, and you get to something new, inspiring and creative. Conversations at this level allow new insights to be discovered, and personal shifts and transformation are totally possible. With this type of conversing and listening, we get to see the whole picture and understand that all of life is dynamic and in process, including your relationship with your son. Many different systems influence an outcome.

In order to reach this type of flow, we spend time developing an open quality of attention, knowing that it will affect others and the field of interconnectedness:

- You can be a channel for newness. You are mindful, centred and calm.
- You allow emergence from the conversation. You focus on the flow and not the outcome.
- You are not looking for problems. You are more positive in an engaging and constructive way. Meaning and contemplation are essential.
- You discover completely new insights. Transformation or shifts are possible.
- You look for the whole picture and understand that everything is dynamic and in process.
- You know that there is such a thing as an energy 'field' – your quality of attention affects others.
- You are open to others and what is not being said or seen.
- You look at what's good for all – co-creating.
- You have more energy and feel inspired.
- You sense your best self and your son's potential.

We are a microsystem within a macrosystem that is sensitive to one another, and aware of and open to other influences.

Ask yourself: *When have you experienced this level of connection?*
With whom and how did it happen?
What is beginning to grow as a result of such conversing?
What have I learnt in this space?

It is only once a boy is particularly mature (in his twenties) that he will fully understand conversing at Level 5. It takes *that* long for the brain to develop!

HOW TO MOVE UP THE LEVELS OF CONNECTION

Have another look at the diagrams for Level 1 and Level 2. When you're stressed, you're going to react at either of these levels. But if you say, 'Let me just take five minutes. I'm going to stop worrying about the family and the problems of the world. I'm going to take a few deep breaths, and calm my body,' is the moment you can begin to relax. And if you calm the body, what messages are you giving the brain? That everything is okay – you're safe.

That is why your granny told you to count to ten when you are stressed. It works! And the reason it does is that this pause gives your prefrontal brain an opportunity to step in and make sense of the situation.

When we are reacting, we often trigger old patterns or moods. There are different levels of awareness and maturity, and none of them are wrong. There is space for each of these. But we have the power to change our attitude and the quality of our attention.

Use an open mind, open heart, open will as a rule of thumb. Ask yourself: 'Am I being open-minded at this time? Can I choose to actually change my attitude or my quality of attention?' Then we could ask ourselves: 'What stands between us right now and a really beautiful moment?' And the answer is: Nothing really. All it requires is a change of heart and mind.

Deep dialogue requires deep listening skills, and to position ourselves at the best level of connection, and we need to understand the different levels of awareness that relate to different levels of maturity. It sounds complex, but it's not. The more mature you become as an adult, the more you are able to progress to a place where you will start saying things like, 'Don't sweat the small stuff' and 'Let's look at the bigger picture' – you start showing expansive awareness:

Can you suspend the voice of judgement and really listen?
What can you become curious about?
What do you appreciate about your son?

When can you practise listening with an open heart and mind?
Can you be more compassionate with yourself?

ARE YOU OPERATING IN THE PAST OR THE 'EMERGING FUTURE'?

In his book *Leading from the Emerging Future: Ego-system to Eco-system Economies* (2013), Otto Scharmer talks about the 'emerging future'. You as a parent are in this difficult situation because *your* son is the emerging future. You are stuck in the past and you only parent in the way you were parented. You are stuck in what is right and what is wrong, what is black and what is white, my way or the highway …

But how on earth are you going to help your son into this emerging future – a future that we don't know much about? We have ideas about it and what is going to happen. We can see the rate of technological development and we know, for sure, that social media is not going to go away.

We have to be in sync with this emerging future, but we cannot know exactly what it will be like. And if we can't know it, then how can we parent for it? By getting creative and realising that the answer is collaborative co-parenting or synergistic parenting – understanding that there will be some things that we are going to be unclear about, unsure about, uncertain about, but coming together as a team to work through them together. Your family then becomes a sanctuary that operates as a team, making allowances for different opinions and ideas. It relies on understanding that the family knows what's best for the members of the family; it also relies on inner wisdom, that there is a deeper place of being that you're able to call upon.

If you have a spiritual leaning or meditative life that is about having compassion and caring for the bigger picture, you will be aware that there is a place we can go to that can really strengthen us, that instils a sense that we have a purpose here and that we just need to get in tune with it. It's an age-old acquiring of inner peace and calm – the point where you find that your happiness comes from within.

DEVELOP INTO A SPIRITUALLY MATURE MOM

We've talked about emotional maturity as the ability to temper your own reaction in order to hear and understand another. But we also have to begin to develop what I call a spiritual maturity.

Spiritual maturity is a greater awareness. We start to consider that our child, our self and our little family unit is a system that is quite dynamic and changeable, but it lives in a community and is affected by the environment around us.

Whether we like it or not, the world is a scary place and the stress it causes affects us all. How we approach and handle that stress help us to cope with the world we live in. If we don't have this ability, the stress can really ravage us. We have to be realistic. We have to make room for the larger environment, but do we put it first? No, we don't. We have to put our calm first.

There is a very real reason why I am encouraging you to start moving into a place where you present yourself with an open heart and a calmer mind, where you are less reactive and more responsive. The reason I'm repeating this is because the latest neuroscience research shows that a tense body switches the brain into survival mode (which happens in the hind- or midbrain). Brain activity during survival mode doesn't connect with the pre-frontal cortex, where our deductive thinking and the setting of intentions are located. Survival mode thus affects your ability to set intentions calmly, and incapacitates your ability to visualise scenarios and play them out in your mind. You're not saying, 'I'm going to this dinner party and I'm going to be nice to my mother-in-law.' Instead, you're operating in the cerebellum – you'll go to the dinner party already tense and, in no time at all, you will want to throw a scoop of ice-cream at your mother-in-law. The survival brain wants only fight or flight or freeze.

Choose to look at the issue from a different perspective. Soften your heart, relax your body, and suddenly everything actually seems better. The most important question a strong mom should be asking herself is: Am I as grounded, sincere and centred as I can be?

WHY EMPATHY IS LOW ON YOUR AGENDA

Who doesn't battle with empathic communication? Most of the time we are tense, so we are in fight-or-flight mode. Empathic communication requires you to slow things down and leave your agenda behind. If you have to have an agenda, the only one you should be worried about is relationship-building. If you put relationship-building first and use your natural resources as a mother to build relationships, you are keeping your son safe.

Our foremost need as human beings is the need for connection. We have a connection-orientated brain; it wants to be in a relationship – with yourself, with your son, with friends, with family ... This need for connection drives us strongly as human beings, and is the most powerful force in a teenager.

At the moment, it might seem as though your son listens to his friends or siblings first. That's a sign that he wants to connect. It tends to go that way for a while – but I found, with my own sons, that it eventually reverts to wanting a good connection with family. However, the relationship has to be there from the start in order for your son to seek reconnection with family.

In the table below, I've illustrated a clear distinction between *doing* things for your son and *being* there for him. Most mothers jump to problem-solving and 'doing'. This is not useful. Teaching him problem-solving, or actioning the plan alongside him, helps him internalise this essential coping skill. Yet first a boy needs help with connecting to his emotions, and needs his parents' support while he figures things out for himself. The emotional support steps I've outlined below will help your son develop his emotional intellect. Practise B; teach your son A.

DOING A: Problem-solving made easy	BEING B: Emotional support steps
1. What is the problem? Stay present, direct and factual	1. Listen
2. How can you (he) solve it? Options: worst-/best-case scenario	2. Mirror
3. What are the consequences? Consequences of each proposed solution: What will happen?	3. Validate: 'It makes sense to me ...'
4. What is the plan? Decide what to do	4. Empathise: 'I guess you're feeling ...'
5. Commit and proceed Take responsibility for this choice	5. Summarise: 'So, what you're saying is ...'
A is the best way to sort stuff out.	B is the best way to stay connected.

Note: Emotional support steps are essential for conflict management. Try these in this exact order.

Sounds of silence

Moms often mention the silences that abound during the teens. Is this something to worry about? Is he unhappy? Is this normal? How do you get a conversation going? How do you find out if he's okay when all you get are grunts or one-word answers?

The first thing to bear in mind is that women and men converse in different ways. We follow a far more circuitous route to get to the point we want to make than men do.

So, when you have an important question to ask, especially one where you're nervous about what the answer might be, pause and think to yourself, 'How can I say this in a very direct way? How can I phrase this as a very direct question?' You might say:

What are you thinking?
What are you feeling?
Why don't you talk any more?

He'll look at you and try to come up with the answer. So, wait for it. You may find you're tempted to give him the answer. Don't! Don't fill the silence with, 'Is there something wrong at school? Is something bothering you?' Stick to a direct, to-the-point question, and then wait. If he can't answer you right away, just say, 'Well, think about it and let me know later.' Full stop.

Keep showing your son the way 'in' to help his self-reflection. In this way, he listens to his own heart rather than being influenced by others' opinions.

Worksheet: Change your communication
PAUSE ... BREATHE ... GROUND

Think of a current concern – a problem your son has. Perhaps he's lazy and you are wondering why he doesn't notice that it is stopping him from achieving his goals. Maybe it's his lack of emotion, or that you don't seem to be communicating much at the moment. Maybe he has a bad relationship with his sister, or he wants to give up maths ...

Here are some questions to reflect on – the answers will help you deepen your dialogue with your son. (It's a good idea to write your answers down.)

1. **What is the key challenge here? What is the concern?** How does your son see it? How does the rest of the family see it?
2. **What is my preferred highest possibility?** Imagine that the outcome is exactly the way you would like it to be, or exactly the way you think he would like it to be. What would that look like? Bring a little vision and insight: 'Is there a possibility that it could look another way with a magic wand?'
3. **Am I lacking some information?** Are you lacking some support? Is there something you need to understand and learn to help yourself in the circumstances, or to help him, or to help your relationship? What is it that you might need to learn that would help the situation? How would an outsider see this situation and what solution would they propose? Do you need some input here? (It might be that you need to get more information, or have a good conversation with an expert or someone who's been there before.)

Worksheet: Homework

Practise the following mantra for effective communication with your son, or for constructive communication in any situation:

I feel ... X ... when you ... Y ... because ... Z ...

- You need all three phrases:
- X – tell him how it makes you feel
- Y – isolate the observable action
- Z – give it a context and let him know how you interpret the situation, or how it impacts on a value you hold dear.

I feel (hurt) when (you don't answer me) because (I feel shut out of your life). I feel (angry) when you (shout at your sister) because (it goes against our family value of caring for each other).

CHAPTER 3

What is conscious parenting?

'My entire approach to parenting is called conscious parenting, which at its core includes mindfulness practices.'

One of the easiest ways to explain conscious parenting is to talk about two opposing messages: one that is intentional and one that is habitual. A habitual parent identifies with their narcissistic ego and with what I call a 'conditioned' mind. This conditioned mind is a collage of beliefs, cultural norms, or the norms that you were brought up with or were taught. Values are often a collection of rights and wrongs, and shoulds and shouldn'ts. If we are lucky, we begin to be aware of this, but most people simply accept the set of beliefs of their culture as 'law'.

When we identify completely with the conditioned mind and ego, it's very easy to parent from a place of fear, and to always worry about what other people think. You may want your children to only succeed according to cultural norms. Are you often anxious and saying things like: 'What if so-and-so sees you?' or 'What will Mrs Jones say?' Or do you use language like: 'You *should do* this and you *must do* that!'? Are you not perhaps raising your teenager more in line with what you or your family thinks is best, as opposed to enabling him to find his own voice and way of doing things? When you only parent in this authoritarian style, a lot of different emotions are triggered, especially anger and frustration – on both sides. A teenager naturally wants to find his own way and, if you prevent this, a boy experiences loads of guilt and shame because he doesn't satisfy your rigid expectations.

If you are *only* worried about your son's performance – in sport, in academics or regarding his manners in public – you can be sure that you are a parent who got stuck in following the norm or an authoritarian mindset.

But there is a conscious and more self-aware approach you can follow. It only happens when you, as a parent, are able to face your internal world in a caring and curious way, as well as being open to change, dynamic growth and being less scared of offending others.

I've come to discover that life is about growth, development and change, and difficult circumstances are always an opportunity for learning: 'up' is a part of 'down', and being down almost always leads to being up. I like to be curious and patient with my sons these days, as opposed to jumping to conclusions, making demands or being impulsive. Aligning to your being and to the being of your son means to stop thinking obsessively and to listen in a deep way. This is real attunement, and it's a tool that can be learnt. Eventually, *doing-fixing-blaming* falls away by itself and makes room for healthy relating.

Being a conscious parent means becoming more self-empowered and finding out how to parent from an authentic love that trusts your inner wisdom and guidance. You can parent from an inner place of calm, while accepting *what is* rather than what others expect. As a conscious adult, you can take responsibility for your behaviour, recognising that you always have a choice. Yet it is also a process of practice. You practise having an open heart, open mind and open will because you value your intention of exploring new ways of thinking and effective ways of connecting with your son and healing your relationship. (See Chapter 10 for more on mindfulness.)

Conscious parenting has the following at its core:
- Being self-aware.
- Being intentional.
- Being authentic and present.
- Living from the IN-side OUT.
- Integrating polarities of good and bad.
- Practising mindfulness.

What do you need to become conscious of to achieve this lofty list?:
- Your thoughts (especially obsessive or judgemental ones).
- Your emotions (especially heightened or habitual ones).
- Your body sensations (especially tense areas).
- Your actions (especially destructive behaviours).
- Your energy (the highs and lows).
- Your soulful prompts (deepest yearnings).

This is a lifetime journey, but most parents want quick fixes. So I often narrow it down to the first steps we can take:

The first step of conscious parenting is to find an intention and a set of values to help you understand the main reason why you parent.

> What are your intentions as a parent:
> - What is the reason you parent?
> - Do you have a clear, short-term parenting intention?
> - What is it to have an overall, long-term intention (what I call an attractor) for the entire journey as a parent?
> - How do you translate this into practice?

Most parents have one aim in mind: to raise a healthy and happy adult. They forget about how their own inner life affects this. We cannot separate who we are from how we parent.

How we approach and live life will influence our parenting. It's about how we treat ourselves and relate to others. It's about how deeply we can love and be loved, and how we are able to commit to others with clear intentions. A more conscious philosophy is the best foundation for our parenting, and only then should we be open to include more information, advice and useful steps.

Parents can become neurotic with shoulds and shouldn'ts, leading them to raise children who may know how to fit in, but miss the essence of life. I have found that parents want tips and strategies, a prescription for 'how to parent'. They want to know if they are doing things 'right', or if their child is 'normal', by ticking boxes on the 'successful parenting list'. Yet this approach is just bobbing on the surface of parenting and, as a result, many children and adolescents feel alienated from others, as well as from their own true sense of self.

After working with hundreds of parents, I have embraced a heart-based approach that transforms how we approach life, how we treat ourselves and how we relate to others. A child almost always wants the following:
- To be seen at an essence level.
- To be heard with a non-judgemental heart.
- To be trusted in an authentic way.
- To be safely connected.

Parenting children is a sacred practice. It is an intense process of opening our hearts as we connect authentically and commit to our sons for a lifetime:

I am committed to supporting my child's self-growth and awareness.
I am committed to attuning to his authentic essence as a human being.

WHAT ARE YOUR VALUES AS A PARENT?

Values are based on the beliefs we hold; they provide us with abstract goals that guide our opinions and actions. We use our values to evaluate people, places or events. Identify what is most important to you in life. Try to find the value that underpins this.

But why values? Because they help us to re-examine our core beliefs and how we judge other families.

As parents, we need to stop for a few minutes, take stock and be more intentional about the values we act out. We need to make choices about those we want to uphold as a family. Inflexible beliefs lead to narrow-minded thinking that alienates us from the next generation. The more we reflect on values, the more open we become to differences. We also need practical suggestions on how to incorporate some of these values in our everyday life.

Although influenced by religion or race, there are common trends that families most aspire to. Examples might be hard work, generosity, contentment, care for the environment, courage, creativity, honesty, inclusiveness, a positive attitude, patience, success, trust, humility, excellence or fairness.

What are your own values and where do they come from? Do you discuss values with your children? Do you talk about the following?:

- How you view marriage and commitment.
- What role religion/spirituality plays in your family.
- How emotionally available you are to others.
- Your beliefs about sharing responsibility.
- Common interests shared by your spouse and family.
- Activities and hobbies you all share.
- How family time is spent.
- How family decisions are made.
- What your family traditions are.

Values and how they are formed run deeper than we realise. The moment your son goes 'off the rails' or is a so-called 'bad influence', the preacher parents appear from the woodwork. And these preacher parents are excellent finger-pointers. Your son's mistakes become your family's fault because you don't have 'good' values or you don't have the 'right' values. Sadly, single mothers often become scapegoats. Can you imagine why?

In all my workshops, I ask parents about their values and they quickly draw up a list, as if those values are part of the fabric of their home. It is only when I ask if these have been discussed and if they have been turned into action that parents pause. It is as if just having a list of values is enough to become good, ethical, moral people. We tend to hide behind our list and criticise those who don't live up to our values.

As a single mother, I experienced this first-hand when I was summoned to the headmaster's office under the pretence of 'We are worried about your son.' It turned out that the headmaster was actually more concerned about me, and the fact that I was dating a younger man who also happened to have long hair. Apparently, this was not a good influence on my son, or his friends! In the meantime, they were having the best time surfing, waterskiing and camping under my partner's vital influence (with me in tow with hot dogs and toothbrushes).

If the headmaster had taken the time to get to know my family, he would have discovered that the fun-filled 'nature connection' my sons discovered in those years was more meaningful than just abiding by institutionally accepted norms.

Having a list of values is just lip service. It does not mean you are *living* that list, and not all values are applicable to everyone. Our lifestyles are dictated by our culture, the activities we love and the circumstances we find ourselves in. Sadly, our deep-seated values are seldom questioned, because they are a product of 'just who we are'.

Research shows that if we do not discuss and continually update our values at different developmental stages in life, they do not stick. (I recommend a family meeting at least once a year.) For values to be integrated into your decisions and behaviour, they need to be supported by your culture, your friends, your stage of life and your personality.

So, coming back to your son, who has 'gone off the rails' – this happens not just because you may have the 'wrong' family values. There are many factors influencing his behaviour, such as his personality, his mental health, substance abuse, his friends, and the fact that teenagers value things like fitting in with their peers, having fun, taking risks and getting attention way more than they do more conservative, accepted values.

Have you ever considered that this stage, called adolescence, has its own values? So, next time you try to force a set of values on your son, pause and consider that those belong to *your* stage of life.

I read somewhere that 'the biggest predictor of how we parent is how we were parented'. This is awesome if you were parented in a kind, secure and loving way, but a disaster if it was critical, judgemental and cold instead. As parents, we most often act out the beliefs and world views that have been passed down by our parents. Values are simply caught, not taught. We seldom stop to choose our own, especially when we are under stress. But you can change this.

Being conscious and intentional in your parenting approach means slowing down enough for self-reflection. But who has time for that? This is what this book is about: a chance to take the time to ponder the way you parent and to set some intentions. *Then* you can decide on the steps to take and a plan to get there. Thinking about your personal, family and son's values is a conduit to conscious parenting.

As parents, we take on the personal responsibility of raising our children with the 'correct' moral, ethical and spiritual values. We decide on how and where children should spend their time, but how much thought do we give to the underpinning values or world views? And here is the trap: If we are fully embedded in a culture that we have not ever questioned, then we only ever see through one cultural lens:

> *You only get somewhere if you work hard.*
> *How you look creates a lasting impression.*
> *What will others say if ...*
> *If you need something done, do it yourself.*
> *Don't boast because people will think you have a big head.*
> *Respect your elders.*
> *If you don't get into university, your life will be a failure.*
> *Money doesn't grow on trees.*

These views then dictate the characteristics we would like to see our son adopt, such as being hard-working and focused. But the big question should be: Do you want to just hand your teen over to the ruling culture?

And now it gets more complicated: I have found that what dads want and what mothers expect of their sons differ. So, culture *and* gender influence our values.

Most dads I have worked with list the following characteristics they would like to see in their sons: assertiveness, drive, success, achievement, self-confidence, entrepreneurial spirit, passion, strength, responsible.

Most mothers wish for the following: fulfilled, good relationship skills, good communicators, a spiritual core, kind, happy, honest, emotionally savvy.

I've noticed that the wish list that dads and moms make are more about their gender preferences than reality. Dads want their sons to succeed in the workplace and list what's called extrinsic values, and moms want their sons to be relational and list intrinsic values. I am not suggesting that this is wrong and that you give up your standards and norms, and just allow your son to surf, have long hair and sing around the campfire. I am asking you to contemplate your world view and your values to check if they were simply 'passed down'. Both this world view and gender bias affect how we want our sons to be in the world, and it all impacts the values that we say are important:

> *What son are you trying to raise?*
> *What is your ideal young man?*
> *What does your list say about you?*
> *Do your values fit the son in front of you?*
> *Are your values appropriate to a teen boy?*

Your home offers a sense of belonging to your son and lays the foundation of 'how' to live in the community. Your home can be that safe place where your son can mature responsibly into young adulthood. Family values can become a guide and a great parenting tool, if we spend a bit of time discussing values and how to live them.

Start by viewing your home as a training ground for 'right living, right thinking, right emotions'. Let it be your choice for a good and wholesome life, and not a set of unquestioned rules simply imposed upon your son. Ask yourself if you are a good example of who you would like your son to be.

For a moment, let's go back to your son who has 'gone off the rails'. Most people who live according to a set of rules, or have a rigid set of values, have what's called a fixed mindset. They are great finger-pointers and preachers. But it's a pretty conservative way to live. A fixed mindset belongs to people who do not challenge the status quo and believe that we are who we are. They see the world as black and white, and normally have a standard list of values that are not questioned. They say these are the 'right' values and others are the 'wrong' ones. Changes or differences are challenging for these people.

Then there are people with a growth mindset. This group is made up of thinkers who say that life is dynamic, and that growth and self-development are essential. This mindset allows for developmental stages, differences and diversity.

According to researcher Carol Dweck, if you have a fixed mindset, you see characteristics as innate. You regard people as either honest, intelligent, kind, etc., or not. It means that if you don't have good traits, you are doomed to fail. A growth mindset, on the other hand, leaves room for change and growth.

What is more important is why your son made the mistake and what he has learnt as a result. Dweck suggests that we apply the little words 'not yet' to the situation. He is not there *yet*. This leaves room for setting goals and developing his character. As a parent, you can then open a conversation with your son about the values he disregarded and what he would do differently in future.

Having spoken to hundreds of parents about their short- and long-term intentions as a parent, I am always struck by a common goal: to raise 'balanced, empathic, communicative children who are also happy, responsible and contributory'. Sound good? Parents' lists are always long and idealised. Yet their message is clear: they unconsciously see themselves as the guardians of the moral life pulse of the community. It's up to them to make their sons listen and obey, as if parents could stamp values onto them.

Have you ever considered that all teens have an internal goodness and an instinct to be who they are, and that this simply needs to be drawn out? Your son longs for his best self to evolve. We can lead by example, creating an environment that is excited about learning and growing, as opposed to discipline and rules being the main focus.

I suggest you model understanding, trustworthiness and self-reflection, and try out a growth mindset when setting your family values. This does come with a caveat: A conscious family is not always a peaceful family. When you understand the value of diverse friends, togetherness and independence, and also embrace change, experimentation, struggle, risk and mistakes, you gain the wisdom of knowing that this is all part of an adolescent growing into his character and finding his own values.

The values also need to be reassessed at different ages. For instance, the first five years of a child's life revolve around establishing emotional security, setting boundaries, exploring, and acquiring positive relationship skills. **For teens, the focus could be on contribution, gratitude, curiosity, self-belief, independence, adventure and conscious conversation/communication.**

If you had to list just five values you feel are important for growing happy, well-adapted children, what would they be? And why?

WHAT ARE YOUR TEEN'S VALUES?

Your son's values are not the same as the family's values. Think about it. Your teenager wants things like independence, exploration, stimulation and fun, and can be appropriately self-centred. This clashes with most family values. I suggest you allow time for him to express his own values, and consider family time together as the time to express family values.

In my course, I have asked some young adults about what values they hope to achieve:

'Honesty, good decision-making skills, fairness, good friendship/communication skills, strong conviction in beliefs.' (24-year-old young man)

'Trust, respect, proactive, self-belief, passion.' (22-year-old young man)

'Confidence, selflessness, positivity, leadership skills, open-mindedness.' (16-year-old girl)

'Exploration, experimentation, responsibility, commitment, contribution, independence, determination, fun, stimulation, friend-time.' (17-year-old boy)

Next time you all sit down for dinner, go around the table and ask everyone for five words that describe their values. Discuss how to make time for personal values and how to action family values. For example: 'On Friday night you can be with friends and have fun, but Sunday is family time.'

I suggest you say to your son, 'We are like a sports team: everyone has a role to play and there are rules of engagement. There is training, there is real life and there is time off, too!' Get his buy-in by finding a language that works.

How values can work

There is a powerful shift that happens when, instead of focusing on the problem, we move our loving attention to our intention, positive values and purpose: your perspective broadens and space unfolds for solutions and a mindful response, rather than impulsive reaction.

Values are a very big part of self-awareness, as well as being a tool for parenting. For example, if you know you value freedom above everything else – freedom of speech, freedom of emotional expression, freedom to be free in your behaviour in your own home – then that's what you are going to fight for. If honesty is something you value very highly, instead of saying, 'I am furious with you right now. I am so angry, I can't even speak to you,' you can say, 'You are going against my value of honesty.' It immediately contextualises your emotion, for you and the person you are interacting with. It lets your kids know what you stand for and what their family stands for. Identify the value, and it becomes a tool that helps you underline for your children what is important to you; it also helps you consciously build family values from your personal values.

I love this values wheel developed by a movement called Common Cause Foundation. I attended their workshop in the UK, where they handed out this wheel of values. It condenses thousands of values into major categories and shows which are the ones that are inherently rewarding (intrinsic), and which require the attention or reward of others (extrinsic). It's important to note that an intrinsically orientated person may also be motivated at times by extrinsic rewards such as personal recognition.

The wheel of values

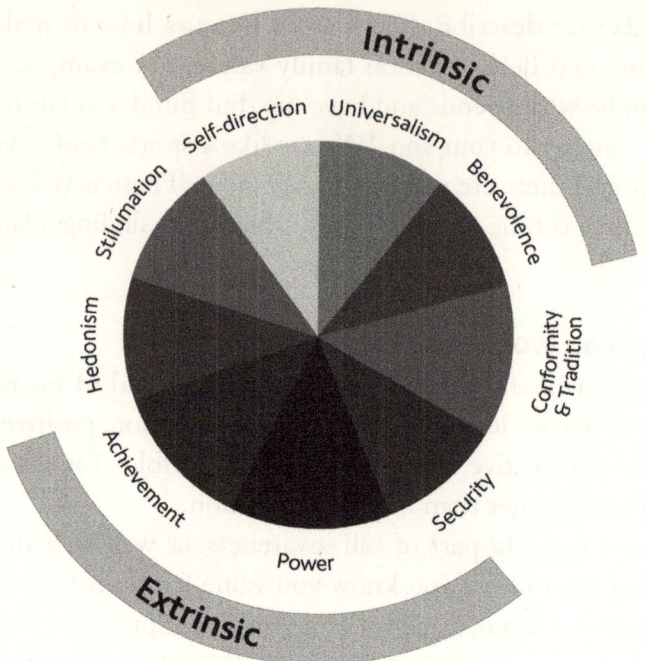

(*Source*: Common Cause Foundation, www.valuesandframes.org)

Research has revealed that opposite values are difficult to hold at the same time, and that the values next to each other blend into each other. In other words, if you are very committed to universalism (peace and equality for all), you may find it difficult to be very power-orientated, whereas achievement and power are more harmonious. Note where your family values slot in and where your son's values lie.

MEGAN'S PARENTING PHILOSOPHY

It's often easier to know a thing by knowing what it is not. When I was studying Vedic traditions of Eastern philosophy, I learnt a process called *neti neti*, which means 'not this, not this'. In other words, one discovers the truth by first discovering what is not true. I developed the following chart based on this principle:

WHAT IS CONSCIOUS PARENTING?

Discovering the conscious path by knowing the unconscious way		
CONSCIOUS	vs	**UNCONSCIOUS**
Open		Closed
Own agency		Others know best
Process-orientated		Outcome-focused
Responsive		Reactionary
Strategic parenting		Copy parents
Self-aware		Habitual patterns
Self-regulates and listens		Blocked to needs of son
Aware of bigger picture		Tunnel vision
Intentional		Only instructional
Non-judgemental/understanding		Criticism, control, competition
Inhabits being		Inhibits doing
Intentional, appropriate		Parenting role-playing
Responsible for own actions		Blaming self and others
Centred and connected		Child- or parent-centred
Other aware		Self-absorbed
Self-sustaining		Needy

All of this starts with the idea that parenting should happen from the inside out. Not the outside in. Basically, change your own energy first and you'll be amazed by how sudden the shifts can happen in your environment, right down to the behaviour of your son.

It's back to that old adage: Focus on *being* rather than *doing*. It does not mean that you can simply put your feet up and set the washing, lift-clubbing and schedules aside. It's remembering that while you are busy doing and fixing, you can still be attuned to 'being'. **It's not what you do, it's how you do it.** This is so important to my parenting philosophy that I could say the reason why I meditate daily is to ensure that I do things from a calm and open place. How I talk and how I behave towards my sons are much more important to me than what I do.

Before you reach out to blame your son for poor performance, check in with your unresolved issues. Before you instruct him, check in with your control issues. Before you shout and yell, check in with your feelings. Before you point fingers at someone else, consider whether you have similar traits. It's all about self-awareness, and it can drive you nuts in the beginning, but please persevere. Being more aware and more open can only improve your relationships. It's pointless spending your entire family life focused on less important matters. A true home sanctuary is one where each family member can be themselves, express love and feel that they belong. For me, being more authentic means I generally enjoy life more and magic happens.

Parenting toolkit

There is no cheat sheet or executive summary for this parenting approach, no matter how much we may wish that there were. Being a conscious parent is a process and a way of life that should last a lifetime. Still, here are some steps to keep on your phone as a reminder:
1. Be open to self-discovery and growth – his and yours.
2. Hold your parenting intention and values close.
3. Calm down and be present. BE, not DO.
4. Have an open heart, open mind and a willingness to engage.
5. Build the relationship, not the problem.
6. Understand teenage development and be attuned to your son's world.
7. Aid him to access his inner (*I can, I am*) and outer resources (*I have*).

WHAT IS CONSCIOUS PARENTING?

Worksheet: Identify your personal and family values

What is most important to you in life? What do you stand for? Use this list to try to identify your personal values:

- a spiritual life
- a world at peace
- love
- true friendship
- unity with nature
- ambition
- success
- status
- adventure
- freedom
- enjoyment
- responsibility
- creativity

- equality
- family security

- health
- honesty
- independence
- inner harmony
- mental growth
- loyalty
- mature love
- meaning in life
- protecting the environment
- respect for tradition
- self-respect
- sense of belonging
- social justice

- wealth
- wisdom

Family values are a little different from personal values, but in the courses I have run I have found family values to be almost identical. Most mothers will list those family values that enhance relationship skills:

- sharing
- caring
- honesty
- loyalty
- fun

- consideration
- sense of belonging
- harmony
- good communication

In contrast, I have found fathers will list family values that enhance life skills:

- ambition
- confidence
- responsibility
- purpose

- success
- focus
- respect

Worksheet: Homework

To help you identify your own family values, consider the following questions:
- What are your family values presently?
- What is your wish list of family values?
- What weakens and what strengthens these? (For example, corporate environment, social media, poor family relationships, education.)
- Which of your values are driven by society/friends? (*I should*.)
- Which of your values are intrinsic? (*I am*.)

A: List **five personal values** that you can live right now:
1. _____
2. _____
3. _____
4. _____
5. _____

B: List **five family values** that are appropriate and possible:
1. _____
2. _____
3. _____
4. _____
5. _____

Compare A and B. Which are the same and which clash? What does this tell you?

CHAPTER 4

7 steps to tackle any parenting problem

'If you are aiming to raise your son well, then raise yourself first.'

In the previous chapter, I wrote about what we need to be conscious of to enable intentional parenting, and the seven steps in this chapter draw from that. These steps increase self-awareness by highlighting your thoughts, emotions, actions and reactions, as well as your intentions. It also includes some helpful mindfulness practices.

It's really easy to react, yet it is a rather unconscious thing to do as a parent. We all have common trigger points that stir up strong emotions and cause us to react impulsively. We are literally hard-wired to *think-feel-react*. In the heat of the moment, emotions rule and it's easy to resort to fight, flight or freeze mode. Our brains are primarily problem-solvers, so when we are in survival mode, we are driven to find problems.

I find that this survival phenomenon leads to narrow-mindedness and judgemental attitudes that only provoke further reactions or a shutdown.

A response, on the other hand, normally comes from a level-headed and rational place once emotions have calmed. A pause offers you a chance to choose a healthy response.

When we are experiencing really strong emotions, we can create space and pause before habitual reactions. This helps us parent from our positive and healthy intentions. So, what to do?

The first step towards being responsive is to simply feel your feelings, and to begin to see them not as a direction to take, but rather as a sign that you need to consider your internal life and focus on what you are really sensing. Secondly, begin to practise self-compassion and be kinder to yourself. Thirdly, develop a metaview skill. As a parent, you need to be able to stand back and see the bigger picture, or at least a different perspective.

One way of doing this is to begin to label your thinking and your emotions. Simply say:

I feel ... and it's causing me to think ...

This immediately gives you a chance to pause and be a little more objective, especially when you feel stuck.

STEPS OF CONSCIOUS PARENTING

Conscious parenting calls on you to be strategic, and to think about the best plan for you and your son in a calm and responsive way. It is calling on you to **respond and not react**.

What is the best way to manage things? What are the consequences? How do we problem-solve? We start to look at issues on a much more rational level. It requires a calm adult, who is much clearer themselves about what resources are available and what needs to be done, to activate the nurturing voice in a parent, instead of the critical voice that is only ever going to trigger rebellion or a stunting need-to-please in your son. This rational, calm voice deflates tense situations and helps lead us towards dialogue. Plus, you give your son the gift of encouraging a calm, rational, nurturing inner voice to make his own.

In the next section, I break this process of conscious parenting down into seven steps to slow you down, take you inward and ensure that you are being conscious of your own self. They are essential steps in any confrontational situation with your teen.

STEP 1: Name it

- What am I feeling? Anger? Rage? Shame? Pain? Frustration? Worry? Guilt? Name the feeling.
- Check into your feelings and body sense. What is this revealing to you? (This is the arena of intuition and embodied experience of the circumstance.)
- Where is this coming from? Be honest with yourself.
- How are you able to witness your own mental/emotional state and accept it without reacting from it? (*I feel the emotions, but I choose to do the right thing.*)

STEP 2: Pause
- Breathe.
- Do not react.
- Do not attack.
- Do not respond.
- Stall.
- Centre yourself.
- Buy yourself time.

A good technique to use at this point is paraphrasing. It buys you time, tamps down your reactivity and also helps you step into the shoes of the other person. You could say something like, 'All right, so what you're saying is that this coming weekend you are going to John's house.' You can literally repeat his words back to him to buy yourself time. It also helps him to hear what he is asking of you.

STEP 3: Acquire some context and information

The next step is to ask a clear question that will elicit more information. Notice that this buys you more time in which to secure your calmness. He will respond – possibly from a place of stress, and possibly in a confrontational way. But he has given you some information, so what do you do next?

Get some bigger-picture information:
- Is this behaviour age-appropriate?
- Is it linked to one of the essential teenage stages he needs to go through right now?
- Does he want to explore autonomy, identity, intimacy or separating from the family?
- What is your teen's deeper agenda?
- What are the needs of this teen?

It is possible that you may engage in a debate where he says something and you say something back – it's a trading of opinions, but there's no empathy, understanding or listening. You are both still reacting and trying to prove that you are right. Instead, focus on his answer to your question. Allow him to come into the conversation. Let your son have a voice. And let his opinion be heard.

STEP 4: What are you assuming?

What are you assuming about yourself, about your son or about the situation?:
- Is this assumption true?
- What are the real facts?
- Can you make space for more information or another perspective?
- Can you observe the facts without your assumptions?

A few classic assumptions of parents:
- He is doing this to irritate me.
- I've told him/warned him about this before.
- He can't be trusted.
- He is manipulating his dad or me.
- What will others think of me/us?
- He thinks the whole world revolves around him.
- He is embarrassing me.
- He should know better.
- He doesn't listen.
- I'm always left to cope on my own.
- I'm a failure at this.
- If I give in now, he'll run amok.
- I always have to fight for what I want.
- He is going to be a useless adult.
- He is the death of me.
- He will have problems with body image.

Think of some other conditioned responses from your own or your mother's repertoire. What emotions do these assumptions generate? Circle the word/s if you find it below.

| Fear of losing control | Anger | Frustration | Worry | Guilt |
| Hopelessness | Disappointment | | | |

STEP 5: Remember your long-term agenda or intention

Remember your main agenda as a parent (to raise a balanced, caring, competent, independent young adult):

- Am I following my overall parenting intention?
- What values am I promoting?
- How will I affect my relationship with my teen in the long term?
- What is the big-picture view for the family or community within which we are embedded?

STEP 6: Be curious, be kind
- What is the energy and influence you are bringing to the situation right now?
- Can you change your mindset and empathise, validate and be curious?
- Do you want to build something here or break it down?
- Does your teen feel heard, recognised and acknowledged?

STEP 7: Handle the practical stuff
Time to draw up a plan of action and encourage your son to problem-solve.

STEP 1–7: Let's recap
- Developing a higher level of emotional maturity than your teen is appropriate here.
- Stay emotionally dispassionate or have empathic detachment if possible.
- Self-regulate or find some distance from the emotions that have been uncovered.
- Put the relationship first, not the problem.
- Focus on the behaviour, not the character.

PARENTING SCENARIO
Let's apply the seven steps to how you could respond to a parenting problem.
Your son says:

I am not taking this. I am leaving and you can't stop me.

As this is happening, it is counterproductive to think about why, what, who, or to find a solution immediately. The situation needs to be experienced first. Be in the experience of the moment.

The best place to start is with your feelings and sensations. Feel your feelings. Feel the sensations surging through you. And try to name the feeling. Is it anger? Is it rage? Perhaps shock?

The toughest thing is **not to react** and rather **witness the passing drama of your feelings**. Pause and breathe. The best grounding technique at the height of this confrontation is to feel your own body, breathe into the stomach, feel your feet on the floor and centre yourself.

Buy time by repeating or summarising what you've just heard: 'So you're leaving immediately?' Now ask the clearest question that is the widest viewpoint you can muster up, in a non-judgemental tone: 'Where are you thinking of going? Do you only hate the current situation, or is there more that has upset you?'

Do not resort to the standard 'closing-down' remark: 'Don't you dare speak to me like that!' There's time for that later. Emotions are running high. Your son is in a 'false-power' phase. This means that his rage helps him to feel powerful in the moment. It's not true power. He is being reactive, angry and defensive, and is literally asking for a confrontation. Do not fall for this teenage power-play game.

Listen to his response and take it seriously. Hear him out and be there for him in the calmest, most centred and grounded way that you can. This is the young male trying to bully you by trying to assert himself.

Check into your assumptions as best you can, and name them. A quick guideline: most of your feelings will be connected to your fight, flight or freeze response, and your assumptions will be a result of your immediate feelings.

If you feel immediate rage, you probably want to take back control and you are fearful that the 'power' is now in his hands. You may be thinking something like: 'I am the parent. He MUST respect me!' This is all about a sudden loss of control, and you are assuming that he is just 'too big for his boots'.

If you are feeling shock, disorientation or bewilderment, it's because it is a new situation for you and you genuinely don't know what to do. You are probably assuming that he may somehow hurt himself or the family. If you feel totally fearful, you are probably assuming that you are helpless, that he is much stronger than you and that all is lost.

From quickly asking yourself what you are feeling and assuming, you can predict your reaction. Will you fight and confront him? Will you take flight and keep quiet or withdraw? Or will you freeze and just stand there like a rabbit caught in the headlights?

The most important thing is that you do not just react from your feelings and sensations. Remind yourself of your core parenting intention. Perhaps it is to facilitate an environment where all members can be themselves to grow and develop appropriately, realising their best potential.

Now, repeat your parenting intention to yourself like a mantra and respond from there:

> *I'd like to assist my son to grow into a fine young man.*
> *We need to grow and develop together.*
> *This is not about me. Let me just widen my view here and change the perspective.*
> *I'm going to pause, breathe, and try to see this from my son's point of view for a moment.*

Then you can choose the right time to ask a very calm question, and then another, and another …

Empathise, validate and really see where he's at and what he's trying to do. Be the adult:

> *I can hear that you are angry and that you really want to go to the party tonight. It seems very important to you.*
>
> *The solution is not just to fight or just leave the house. Let's try to work it out, because it has become very important now.*
>
> *You are really asserting yourself and I'm finding it scary/confrontational/ overwhelming. Can you take some time to calm down and I will too, and then we can talk again?*
>
> *I'd like to understand you, and I hope you can listen to my viewpoint, too. Let's leave it for now and talk again in a bit.*
>
> *Hopefully we can talk when our emotions have settled and we can problem-solve practically and maybe come to a compromise.*

The biggest learning curve for teens is when they do something that actually takes them out of their depth. For example, he goes to the party and agrees to some boundaries and a pick-up time. Or he does not and he leaves the house. He has to deal with the consequences, and we have to try to keep him safe while he spreads his wings.

But spread his wings, he must.

What do teens really need?
They need to be seen as they are; to be enjoyed; to be affirmed or validated. They have a longing for their natural, intrinsic nature to be seen – a kind of soul-sensing. They want relational attunement.

What is a parent's real role?
- To give sound, balanced advice.
- To be a good role model and be that person that they expect of their teen.
- To lead the way in a good, true and kind way.
- To coach in a firm, clear, yet fair way.
- To strive to do what they say they will do.
- To be able to see and encourage a teen's true strength, capacity and natural talents.
- To give up expectations and to truly attune to a teen's real self.

What does a teen love to do?
He is longing for his 'life'. He loves to feel it and express it. He wishes to experience his unique life force and personal 'power'. He wants to expand, fulfil his potential and grow up. He wants to be good at something, to master it and stand out. Yet he also wants to fit in and be a part of the group.

What holds a teen back?
- His frail ego and self-consciousness.
- A fear of getting hurt and making mistakes.
- Continual comparisons to others his age.
- His inexperience, combined with a desperate urge to be a man.
- Stereotyping.
- A need to fit in and to please.
- A feeling of not being worthy or good enough.
- Others' demands on him to perform.

BEING A 'COACH' MOM

As a mom, your agenda needs to revolve around building relationships. Part of your job, from now on, as a mother to a teenager is to develop skills. So you become 'Coach' Mom: you are teaching life and social skills; you've done manners to death, so let that go. Instead, focus more on the quality of the relationship he has with his friends and his school. What does loyalty mean to him? Focus on building skills like resilience. Connecting with him will only come from empathic *listening* techniques. It will not come from your problem-solving default.

In terms of building resilience, these are your mantras:

I get you.
I trust you.
I encourage you.

Planting these ideas helps him to build an attitude of *I can, I have* and *I will*:

I CAN is an attitude of self-confidence that says he believes in his own abilities and personal agency; it's validating a sense of 'I am'.

I HAVE is about what resources he can use and how his abilities can be turned into action.

I WILL is the actual action and represents the 'will' and courage to proceed. Somehow, as coach, we need to encourage this fragile will and not focus on the outcome, because it's all about the effort and the experience of the journey, not the end goal or reward.

Keep saying things like:

You've got this.
You know what to do.
Listen to your gut.

This will help your son to develop resources like resilience and a positive attitude so that he can say:

I have resources.
I have inner strength.
I have confidence.
I have skills that I can use.

In this way, he can solve his own problems from a position of confidence and resilience.

While problem-solving comes easier for us, from now on, think first about building his skills. First, you connect with him in the moment:

I hear you.

Then you ask:

What do you think is going to be the best plan of action?
How are you going to set about this plan?
Tell me what needs to be put into place.

Lastly, there must always be a follow-up:

How did that go?

Then, check that he is problem-solving.

Often, your son won't do it – he won't do what he said he was going to do, because it is something new and it is going to take time for him to get used to it. For so long you have been telling him what to do, and now you are going to start handing him some responsibility.

You might say to him, 'I hear that you're worried about maths. What can you do about it? Do you think extra lessons will help? Okay, so let's arrange some extra maths lessons. Find out who Johnny goes to.' Of course, you don't stop being a mother. Maybe you're going to have to get the tutor's number and schedule a time and sign your son up. But you are still teaching him problem-solving skills and the steps that he can take. Most importantly, during the conversation, your focus is on listening. When you talk, it's only to prompt a solution from him. This is what I mean by coaching.

Never forget, it is always fine to pull parental rank. There is definitely a place for it and times when it is the appropriate response – but it's all about balance. And though it's a good thing to calm down and talk through the event and the behaviour, when a non-negotiable line has been crossed, you have to make it very clear that his behaviour is unacceptable and that there will be consequences.

In order to move into a dialogue, you need to be able to put yourself in his shoes, and that means seeing things through his eyes. What's important to your son? What's important for a thirteen-year-old or a sixteen-year-old? What is his life about? How does he experience his life? What is going on in that developmental stage?

At age thirteen or fourteen, it's all about identity for them. What does this search for self actually mean? He's trying to discover who he is. How is that showing up for your son?

You really have to take the time to be curious and observe what it is that your son really likes: what's his favourite food, colour and activity? Where does he feel happiest? What brings him joy? What makes him feel insecure?

Begin to explore this curiously because, believe me, he is completely different from the little boy at age six, seven, eight or nine. You will be surprised by how much the little boy you knew will differ from the eighteen-year-old man he'll become. It is remarkable how tastes, preferences and ideas can change. He could go from a hyperactive, attention-deficit little boy of six to a very steady nineteen-year-old, and you'll just wonder how on earth that happened. It's because the brain develops at such a rapid pace from the age of sixteen that you will be dealing with someone almost new.

As mothers, we feel that we know our sons intimately, and yet they're changing under our noses. Be sensitive, be empathic, be curious about who your son is. What is his temperament? His nature? The only way to discover this is to be present and observe.

Parenting tips from the therapist's couch

When all else fails and you feel lost, shocked or unsure of what to do as a parent, there are three sure-fire attitudes to practise and develop:

#openmind 💡
#openheart ♥
#openwill 🧝

1. **To be open-minded is a non-judgemental and non-critical approach and takes a wider view.** It means you are prepared to listen to your teen's opinions and ideas in a fresh way, unclouded and unfettered by your own agenda. An open mind is holistic and is interested in the process rather than just looking for an outcome. It helps to lessen expectation and an ego-driven outcome.
2. **The open heart is more easily understood when considered from its opposite.** A closed heart is cold, mean, petty and unforgiving. So, to be open-hearted means that you are available, empathic, warm and generous. You are generally more accessible.
3. **The open will is a willingness to be present to where your teen is at.** It's about showing up, seeing things through his eyes, and purposefully engaging and 'leaning in'.

All three positions together create a metaview skill: being able to shift from a narrow focus or tunnel vision to the broader context. From content to context, and back again. This takes us out of pettiness and judgement, so that we are open enough to discover what is good and positive, no matter what the circumstance. It helps us become a participant in our teen's life, and to engage, experiment and enjoy the moment.

This shifts us from being the parent in control, to the parent who is 'with' and alongside a child. An open mind, open heart, open will increases acceptance of a teen's needs, and we develop a deeper quality of relationship, so that trust is formed.

We can all start this practice immediately: open your mind to hear new ideas; soften your heart; and be willing to lean in and listen!

WHAT YOUR BOYS ARE TELLING ME (AND THAT YOU NEED TO KNOW)

I always ask high-school boys for any advice they would like to give their moms:

'For me, communication died out a bit. I think my mom felt like I didn't really care about her that much because I wasn't constantly talking to her, but it's not true. I am not a very communicative person, so I like to keep to myself quite a lot. My mom knows I love her but I don't really express it that much. That is something that some mothers could learn about their son – that they don't show their love for you so much as they did in prep school, but the love is there.'

'I feel like you just need to make sure that when you discuss topics, like the alcohol thing, make sure that your son can tell you anything with you taking it in and speaking to him in a mature way. If he questions like, "Why can't I do it if I choose to in moderation?", don't shut him down straight away. In prep school, a lot of the time I did what my mom said I had to do and now I'm asking more questions – you have to keep an open mind and really communicate – respect him in what he says and get to a mutual standpoint. Don't shut down your son's conversation.'

'I think the main thing that I have taken from my relationship with my mom is that consistency is the number-one thing that I think that I appreciate about my mom. No matter what I have done, I always know that I am going to get into trouble or I know that it will be a positive reaction. It's not like I'm unsure if I want to tell my mom. It goes back to the thing about trust, and I think trust and consistency go hand in hand.'

'Sometimes me and my mom don't see eye to eye, so it could lead to arguments despite my maturity. That is just one thing that has happened to me recently. It's something that can happen and be aware of it. There can be opposition at this point as you are growing.'

'Listen to each other before making a rash decision to shout. Just sort of keep it cool so he can trust that he can come to you and you won't immediately shout it down, so he will know that he can always tell you something, otherwise he won't come to you. So listen.'

'Personally, when I am at the boarding house I am completely on my own and, when I go home, I'm not used to having my mom always telling me what to do. Sometimes I get really angry at her telling me to clean my room. At the boarding house I do it myself and I don't need my mom to tell me to do it. She shouts at me to do this and to do that and sometimes I just go mad. My advice is, they will do it by themselves if you just don't bug them. The more she tells me to clean my room, the less I will do it.'

> **Worksheet: Being a present and intentional parent**
>
> Journal on the following statements:
> - As a mom, my short-term goals for my son are …
> - My overall long-term goals are …
> - I chose to be a parent because …
> - I am promoting my goals when I am …
> - I am limiting or neglecting my parenting goals when I …
> - I am most satisfied as a mom when …
> - I am most dissatisfied as a mom when …
> - My relationship with my son has been … and now is …
> - I get positive responses from my son when I …
> - I get negative responses from my son when I …
> - The ideal parent should …
> - The things I worry about the most as a parent are …
>
> My parenting partner:
> - Our parenting conflicts are usually about …
> - We could make the following adjustments …
> - My frustrations and joys about my partner's parenting approach are …
> - This impacts me in the following way …
>
> My parents (when I lived with them):
> My mom was most helpful when …
> I wish she would have …
> The ways my dad influenced me were …
> The things that had a negative impact on me were …
> I would like to be like them in this way …
> I do not want to copy the following …

Worksheet: Homework

I did some training in Imago therapy many years ago that centres on the idea that many of our childhood wounds come from the way our parents 'shut us down' or limited our expression. I created this table for mothers to notice where they might be limiting their son's expression. It's a table for self-reflection and not a psychological assessment:

Rate your parenting challenges	Never 1	Little 2	Sometimes 3	Mostly 4	Always 5
I support my son's ability and freedom to think					
I support the expression of ALL his feelings					
I allow him to be playfully physical					
I allow him to enjoy movement and his body appropriately					
I calmly manage his noise, activity and boisterousness					
I support ALL his creative tendencies					
I always allow him to be who he is at home					
I pay attention when he needs me					
I allow him his privacy					
I am consistent with my parenting					
I am able to set limits and abide by them					
I assert my personal boundaries					
I respect my son's personal boundaries					
I deal calmly and appropriately with his incessant needs and wants					
I manage my anger and frustration well					
I listen to and validate my son's opinions, ideas and concerns					
I empathise with him					
I allow him to explore the world					
I communicate well and reflect					
I spend time with him alone					
I am confident that I know which behaviours are appropriate					

I allow him to have and be with friends					
I am flexible with 'rules' and manners					
I feel connected to him					
What have you now learnt about yourself as a parent?					

CHAPTER 5

Who is this boy?! Understanding the stages of development

'We all come into the world hard-wired to grow, connect and fit in. Your son is no different.'

The reason teen boys often become difficult between the ages of thirteen and fifteen is the many bodily, emotional and psychological changes they are going through. It is a time of tumultuous change, where there are external and internal influences at work. Yes, friends and the media influence his behaviour, but so do his temperament, genes and hormones.

Testosterone begins to have an influence and, as women, we don't have first-hand experience of this. We are women and female, raising boys towards manhood with their different hormones, priorities and needs. We have no experience of boyhood/testosterone/masculinity and a man's world.

Mothers are generally excited to see their young men brimming with testosterone, energy and boisterous enthusiasm, yet are frustrated and hurt when they display surliness, aggression, rudeness and lethargy. Moms want their sons to express emotions and have respect for girls and women, yet they've become monosyllabic! It is a challenge for every mother: Can you allow his developing masculinity and yet stand your ground against his overly assertive behaviour?

It requires some understanding and insight from us. He is developing from a boy into a man. His biology is directing the obvious physical and mental changes, yet he is also affected by society's messages of what it is to be a man.

The hormone testosterone changes the brain. Logical and concrete thought is available to teen boys, yet during a sexual encounter or strong desire the executive functioning of the brain seems to be bypassed momentarily. It is as if the new sexual urges slow the brain's higher functioning capacity and poor judgement may be exercised. Neuroscience confirms that an adolescent's judgement can be overwhelmed by the urge for new experiences and thrills, and this includes sexual impulses. They sometimes seem driven to seek experiences that produce strong feelings and sensations.

When psychologists start looking at teenage development, we think about milestones and the tasks that teenagers need to complete to reach maturity – to obtain the competencies and the skills for an independent, adult life.

Where before your son saw himself in terms of a collective identity – one of the family – he is now moving towards his own identity. This is his developmental task as a young teenager, and everything plays into it. As you did when he was five years old, you are going to deal with boundary testing now – this is him forming his identity around discovering what is important to him.

Remember that if your son questions what you believe in, it is not a rejection of you or your values; it is part of a process of searching for his own identity and flexing his newly found mental muscle.

This process is going to happen, no matter what. All boys go through it. You cannot hold him back, but it helps to understand what is going on.

DEVELOPMENTAL PHASES OF TEENAGERS

Remember the events you watched out for when your son was a baby – sucking, smiling, grabbing, sitting, going onto solids? These are milestones you didn't have to chivvy along – it's a natural progression. The following are the early behaviour and developmental phases:

- 0 to 2 years – attachment (physical connecting)
- 2 to 3 years – exploration (emotional security, exploring, coping with change)
- 3 to 4 years – the first throes of identity formation (differentiation, playing with personas)
- 4 to 6 years – the beginning of certain competencies (belief in personal power, socialising)
- 6 to 9 years – the development of empathy and concern for others (understanding friendships).

Your son reached all of these milestones. There is going to be a repeat of these same patterns during the teen years, but obviously at a more intense level. And you don't have to do anything to make them happen. What you can do is make room for them.

Remember when your son was a three-year-old boy, you made space for his exploration? Maybe you put your Tupperware in a place in the kitchen where he could open the cupboard and dig in, you put locks on other cupboards and you moved the breakables to a higher shelf ... You understood that it was a developmental phase, and you adapted to make it easier for both of you.

Teenage developmental phases are less easy to handle, because we aren't in control. On top of that, teens are very free with their criticism, often complain and have mood swings.

But the process is easier if we understand what the milestones are during this tumultuous time of change from dependence to independence.

Milestones of early adolescence (age 11 to 14)

Milestone	Teen behaviour	Effect on family
Worries about his developing body	Very self-conscious Compares himself to others	Parents see this as self-obsessed
Hormonal changes	General moodiness Gentle boys may become more aggressive Develops acne	Parents find surliness hard to live with
Asserts independence and wants to be an individual, not 'just one of the family'	Experiments with dress, speech, manners, etc., to have a separate identity	Parents feel rejected and have difficulty accepting their son's need to be different
Rebellious, defiant behaviour	Risky choices and gets in trouble	Parents dislike the rudeness and find it tough to keep up a good relationship
Strives for autonomy	Demands more freedom	Parents have difficulty finding a balance between freedom and overprotection
Friends become most important	Identifies as closely as possible with friends by having the 'right' clothes, hairstyle, etc., listening to the same music	Parents find copying or cloning irritating and financial demands increase
Needs to feel a sense of belonging to a peer group: boys form gangs	Holds friends (and friends' parents) up as a yardstick for demands	Parents are suddenly compared or criticised

Milestones of middle adolescence (age 15 to 16)

Milestone	Teen behaviour	Effect on family
Becomes less self-absorbed and develops greater ability to compromise	More composed, equable and tolerant. Can accept others' opinions	Parents gradually find that their son is becoming easier to live with
Learns to think independently and makes his own decisions	Reluctant to let parents interfere or control his life. Less suggestible and less eager to conform. More discriminating. Friends are still an influence	Authoritarian parents battle unless they learn to be less controlling and trust their son
Experiments continually with self-image	Clothes, hairstyles, attitudes and opinions change frequently	Parents who take these frequent changes of image too seriously will worry too much
Needs to collect new experiences, test boundaries and take risks	Likely to experiment with cigarettes, alcohol and soft drugs	Anxiety rises for parents, especially about risks, and decisions about how and when to set limits need to be discussed
Self-consciousness recedes	More sociable. Less shy	Teen is prepared to mix with parents' friends
Starts to build up a set of values and to develop a personal sense of morality	Questioning (and possibly setting aside) ideas and values of the family or home religion	Can lead to conflict in the home if the teen rejects attitudes/beliefs that the parents value highly
Deepens intimate friendships and makes good friends	Wants to spend less time with the family and more time with friends	Parents worry about influence of friends and resent being 'treated like a hotel'
Accepts own sexuality and forms sexual relationships that involve intense and new feelings	Starts dating. Guards privacy and may seem secretive. Intimate relationships may be short	Parents' anxiety about their son's safety and the 'need to know' may become too intrusive

Milestones of late adolescence (age 17 to 18)

Milestone	Teen behaviour	Effect on family
Idealistic	Attempts to find a social or political cause to be committed to May turn to religious cults or movements	Parents may be distressed at the rejection of their religion or beliefs
Involvement with life, work and relationships outside the family	Must learn to cope with the stresses this inevitably brings Will probably want to go away with friends instead of joining in the family holiday	Parents' natural wish to protect their child may cause friction Parents may have the chance to enjoy the kind of holiday they want, without having to take anyone else's wishes into account
On a course to achieve financial or emotional independence	Anxieties or uncertainty about the future can wreak havoc with temper, confidence and self-esteem Stress increases	Parents may still be financially supporting an adolescent who is not emotionally dependent on them (can make for an uneasy and unequal relationship)
Becomes more able to form stable sexual relationships	Likely to have a serious girlfriend or boyfriend and to spend more time with her or him	Parents tend to worry about a too early or too serious commitment and fear that schoolwork may suffer
Feels an adult on equal terms with the family	Tends to feel he has insights into and experience of the world that parents may lack	Parents may find themselves being condescended to and resent this role reversal (may even be intimidated)
Almost ready to become an independent and self-reliant adult	May want to leave the family home and find a place of his own Dependencies are hated	Parents' own relationship may need some readjustment with their teen leaving home

Your son is changing, and you cannot stop it. Where before you were in control and he was following the rules, now he is exercising his own control and applying his own rules. He is moving towards self-determination, self-discipline and self-motivation.

The most important process that is happening here is personal growth, which you cannot turn into a project, just as you couldn't turn the ability to stand up into a project for a baby: he is going to stand when he is going to stand, and when he has the physical strength to do it!

From being told what is right and wrong, your son is now developing his own values and making his own choices, and we have to allow room for that.

But how are you going to parent a more emotionally mature boy who is going through all these neurological, hormonal and emotional changes?

Newsflash – you don't have to parent that! You just have to lead by example, and wait for the signs that his brain is developing and the emotional/limbic system is finding its balance with the prefrontal cortex. You can help him identify his feelings. If he complains of a sore tummy, you know it may mean that he is anxious: 'Have you thought that maybe you are actually worried about something?' You keep directing him back to his inner world so that he can learn to trust it.

THE TEENAGE BRAIN IS NOT A FULLY FORMED BRAIN!

It is important to realise that, in the teenage brain, the prefrontal cortex hasn't developed all its neural connections yet. The growth of the cortex into the prefrontal cortex (behind the forehead) is still happening. The prefrontal cortex has many functions, but those pertinent to teens control the following:
- Deductive and analytical thought.
- Being reflexive and aware of consciousness.
- Thinking about your own thinking.
- Being able to anticipate consequences.
- Being able to set long-term goals and intentions.

In general, the prefrontal cortex controls self-control and self-awareness. It is also the most important phase of spiritual development. To be able to be self-aware is only possible once brain activity begins to move into the prefrontal cortex. True compassion can only happen once the prefrontal cortex can cope with the 'fight and flight' limbic system – once your son is able to use his emotional sensors to calm himself.

You can only set an intention in this part of the brain. In ancient Vedic wisdom, the ages thirteen to sixteen mark the move into a higher consciousness – that of self-awareness within a broader belief in God.

As your son enters his teens, he is not likely to be able to set a mature intention and see it through like an adult. For example, say you are going to a dinner party with a bunch of people you really don't like or get along with. You set an intention – you say to yourself, 'I am going to be nice and relaxed and get through it.'

The only way you can do this is by using your developed prefrontal cortex. Without it, you'd be in fight-or-flight mode and you'd be sitting there thinking, 'What a stupid, silly idiot.' The next minute you'll react and be rude, or you'll decide that you couldn't bear it a moment longer and leave. A fully developed prefrontal cortex is the only thing that can monitor thoughts, feelings and actions, and can calm you down.

If you put a young teenager through an MRI machine, the limbic system is the part of the brain that will be firing the whole time. Teens are highly stimulated and reactive. Take the screaming that goes on with girls from age ten into the early teens. You think that there is an intruder in her room and rush up there, and it's a little spider in the corner! Their reaction is a function of high energy and heightened emotions: in a young teen boy, it can show up as acting out and in risk-taking, but as boys go further into their teen years, brain connectivity will move towards the prefrontal cortex – the limbic system starts calming down and the executive functions of the prefrontal cortex start taking over and having a say.

Along with the milestones listed in the tables on pages 85 to 87, your teenager is also going to go through their early developmental stages again. Remember attachment, the stage for 0 to 2 years?

Now his desire for intimacy is driving a need for attachment all over again. He will text a girl or have WhatsApp interchanges with his mates all the time because his brain development is triggering a desire for attachment, and as parents we need to understand this. Attachment theory claims that our early attachment experiences impact all our relationships, even into adulthood (including how we relate to our teens). It is how we bond with and befriend others.

There are three attachment styles: secure, ambivalent and avoidant. A teen who has experienced *secure attachment* (he felt secure, soothed, safe, and seen by you and/or his dad in the first two years of his life) will enter new relationships with positive expectations and healthy boundaries. *Anxious attachment* styles are always fraught with drama and high emotion, accompanied by a push-pull pattern. *Avoidant attachment* is just that: he will prefer independence to a close-knit nest.

The most exciting aspect of attachment theory is the thorough research and advice it offers. Sue Johnson, award-winning psychologist and author of *Hold Me Tight* (2008), who found an emotionally centred approach to relationship therapy called EFT, says that we are social mammals who survive and thrive by bonding and belonging. And it's never too late to learn how to grow and heal through authentic attunement with a significant other.

Dan Siegel, clinical professor of psychiatry and author of *Brainstorm* (2013), a book dedicated to understanding the teen brain, reminds us that we have a relational brain and that all development (especially as a teen) happens in relationships. Your son's family life is important for his mental and emotional health, no matter how hard he seems to be pulling away. Yet he also needs emotional attunement. This means that he needs to be heard and seen for who and what he is. According to Siegel, this helps with brain integration and calms the nervous system.

As mothers, we need to get real and not live within our expectations of what should be. Relate to your son at his level and, if that's too tough, seek help or therapy. As parents, we can learn how to nurture, empathise and truly listen to our teens without trying to fix, advise, control or manipulate. Just being there with an open heart and mind is enough. He may not talk that much, but verbal communication is not the only way to love and connect.

The other developmental tasks your son will be occupied with include independence, autonomy, freedom, individuality, individuation and identity formation. It's a bit like the toddler phase of exploration happening all over again. This time around you are not moving vases, but alcohol, out of his reach!

He also needs to understand and deepen his maturity around morality, so he can form good, strong relationships and eventually start his own family. His big question now is, 'Who am I?'

WHO IS THIS BOY?! UNDERSTANDING THE STAGES OF DEVELOPMENT

During this stage, you cannot control his physical development, and you may not be able to control his natural temperament, which affects his emotional development. What you can be involved in is to help him with his developmental tasks.

But it's not always easy …

> ### Worksheet: Homework
> Ask yourself the following questions about your own 'developmental' stage:
> - Are YOU autonomous and independent?
> - How would you describe the developmental stage you are in?
> - What are the benefits and challenges of this stage?
> - Are you sure about and secure in your own identity?
> - What attachment style have you exhibited in your relationships?
> - Have you noticed whether you are avoidant or too clingy?
> - Can you attune to another and empathise?

CHAPTER 6

Things all boys must learn

'Follow your bliss and don't be afraid, and doors will open where you didn't know they were going to be.'

– Joseph Campbell, *The Hero with a Thousand Faces*, 1949

Your teenage son is searching for his identity. This search is driven by exploration and, once he has defined it, he will hopefully commit to it for life. The exploration starts between the ages of thirteen and fifteen:

What hairstyle do I want?
What music do I listen to?
What group do I hang out with?
Am I an extrovert or an introvert?
Am I popular, or not?
Who am I in this group?
Who am I in this school?
Am I gay? Am I straight?

These questions are all part of exploring his true identity, and he will only commit to it when he's explored it sufficiently. This takes a certain level of maturity.

One day he might like spaghetti bolognese; the next day he's a vegetarian. One week he may vehemently say, 'I'll never smoke an e-cigarette. Vaping is not my thing.' Next, you catch him with it in his hand.

And we get hysterical!

Even if we manage to keep calm, we're asking questions like, 'Where is your commitment? Where is your sense of responsibility?'

You need to know that commitment will not happen until much later in his development. The actual formation of identity requires a lot of exploration before a commitment to ideals and identity is reached. There will be a lot of times when you are disappointed and wonder what's going on. It takes time for an identity to form. Eventually, we all get to a point where we trust ourselves to do what we say we are going to do. When he gets to the age of thirty, we will hopefully see a real commitment to the person he says he is, but, as you know, humans never stop growing. All you can be sure of is that, as a teenager of thirteen to fifteen, his conception of himself is very much in flux, and will be for some years to come.

Relax, you have a normal teen boy in the house! Adolescence has been described as that hideous period when children undergo personality changes and become argumentative, rebellious, defiant, confrontational and uncooperative. The tension, friction and conflicts that accompany the onset of adolescence are unavoidable. In fact, they are essential and a normal and healthy part of your son's development.

I'm going to help you create the platform for his autonomy to expand safely, for him to explore and find his identity, freedom, independence and intimacy, and to develop his own morality. These are the major developmental tasks of adolescence. You need to help your son, in your own way, to negotiate these tasks and successfully accomplish them. His maturity and psychological well-being depend on it. You need to understand the five things your son is exploring:

1. He needs to find his autonomy.
2. He needs to separate from the family.
3. He needs to explore intimacy and sexuality.
4. He needs to explore identity.
5. He needs to find his tribe (group or clan).

In other words, healthy adolescent development requires that teens successfully accomplish some important tasks. They need to experience some control over their lives, experiment with and explore an autonomous identity, and begin to experience some independence from family constraints. Being bombarded by surges of testosterone marks their entry into sexuality and relationships.

A TEENAGER'S FOUR STEPS TO INDEPENDENCE

While my boys were still at school, I ran a course for mothers on an ongoing basis and worked very closely with school counsellor Jason Bantjes, who wrote his master's thesis on masculinity and societal beliefs. Together, we wrote up the four steps below, and they became my creed for mothers in all my workshops. We did draw on many of the top researchers in developmental psychology and gender studies at the time, such as Erik Erikson, John Bowlby, Lawrence Kohlberg, Steve Biddulph, Michael Gurian and William Pollack, so these developmental stages are well documented. I am, though, forever indebted to Jason for helping me formulate these steps so clearly.

I always tell mothers: 'They [your sons] may appear to be surly, rude, unavailable or totally into sex, yet they are truly trying to achieve something. They are not simply against you; they have to perform certain tasks to progress to maturity. This is *really* what your boys are up to.'

None of these steps that your teenage son needs to take to become an independent adult can be bypassed.

STEP 1: He needs to gain control (autonomy) over his own life

Your teenager needs to enter adulthood knowing that he has some control over his life and decisions. Yet he will need to acquire the confidence and necessary skills to make his own decisions and to accept that his actions will have consequences that he will have to live with.

Many of the arguments that you and your son have are nothing more than an attempt on his part to **achieve autonomy** over his own life. Welcome these as signs that your son is maturing and endeavour to help him learn the skills he needs to problem-solve and regulate his reactions and impulses. Your son needs your approval, love and support, no matter what he says, *and* your guidance to temper his impulsive actions. Some ideas for helping him with this important task are the following:

- Do you see him starting to take control of his life, and taking responsibility for his actions and their consequences? Let him take control of his room – make sure he has a space that is his alone. Don't set up a revision timetable for him when exams roll around – let him take responsibility and control. Offer help if he needs it, but let him do it himself.
- Give your son clear but reasonable limits. He needs to know where the boundaries are. Limits provide your son with security and safety,

and allow him to make informed decisions. Negotiate freedom within boundaries.
- Try to create opportunities for your son to make his own decisions and practise being autonomous. This might include, for example, managing his own finances and buying his own clothes and toiletries.
- Be available to listen and guide when help is asked for, but step back whenever possible. Coming to your son's rescue unnecessarily or prematurely may suggest that you don't believe in him.
- Freedom comes with responsibility. He needs to stick to agreements or commitments. Hold him accountable more than ever before.
- Tolerate as much independence as you can (without a GPS tracker) and remember that your son is not rejecting you, he's just growing into himself. If most of your arguments start or end with him saying, 'Why do you always treat me like a child?', then independence is probably an issue.
- Accept your limitations. You cannot force your teenager to work harder than he wants to. You can only make sure that he knows the consequences of what he is doing.

STEP 2: He needs to establish his own identity

Your son needs to enter adulthood with a reasonable self-image (not perfect, but okay). He needs to be aware of his strengths, weaknesses, values, goals and beliefs, and to perceive himself as being a unique and valuable member of his community. He needs to feel that others accept and respect him for who he is. To achieve this, your son will challenge the things you say, the values you hold and your opinions. This is not a rejection of you; it is part of a process of searching for his own identity. A grounded identity requires that he stand on his own two feet and find his voice.

Think about your son. Name one incident you've noticed recently that points to him trying to **develop his identity**. It could be that he's working hard at school because he defines himself as 'the clever one', or maybe he's not working hard because he defines himself as 'not bothered about marks'. How are you going to parent that?

Maybe he's insisting on certain clothes or a trendy haircut… How do we allow him to form his identity safely in these areas? Are neat hair and clothes a non-negotiable for you, or could you compromise, say, by allowing him to do whatever he likes with his hair during the holidays, but not during term time? Could you allow him some freedom with his personal appearance, because it is the safest place to start exploring his identity?

The flip side of this search for identity is the importance teenagers place on how others see them. It can definitely influence their vision of self.

Think of examples from your son's life and how you can make space, or where you absolutely will draw the line.

- Remember that your son is an individual, not merely an extension of you. Do not expect your son to share your dreams, ambitions and values; he has his own. Are you trying to raise a 'mini-me', or a unique human being?
- Aid him in building his self-esteem, but also by believing that he can work things out for himself. Expect him to blame and project due to his fragile and immature ego.
- He may experiment with different identities via clothes, language or music, and may even closely follow specific group behaviours – this is all normal.

STEP 3: He needs to liberate himself from the family

Your son needs to feel that he is part of the family, but at the same time be allowed some separation from it. Much of your son's challenging adolescent behaviour stems from an attempt to perceive himself as his own man who is distinct from his family (while still having a role to play in the family).

Where is he setting himself apart? Is it in an opinion, or in his room, or by making arrangements without telling you or asking you, or by ordering his siblings around? In some boys it will show up in silence – he just closes the door or puts his headphones on and locks himself in.

Understand that your son will start to look outside of the family unit for emotional support, approval, recognition and acceptance. This is a normal part of growing up. If you attempt to limit this behaviour, you may force him to **liberate himself** from the family in a way that is painful for everyone.

Be more self-aware, especially of what your own identity and goals are, and find interests outside your son's life. It's time to get a life (back). This can be scary for moms of young teens. Yes, he is going to leave you, and you are going to help him to do that by encouraging him to explore these different aspects of his teenage years.

Remember that your son's questioning of what you believe is not a rejection of you; it is part of a process of searching for his early manhood or adulthood.
- Encourage your son to spend time with other families.
- Help your son identify adult role models or mentors.
- Allow your son's voice to be heard and listen to his opinions, especially if they are different from yours.

STEP 4: He needs to explore and understand intimacy

You'll see obvious development in this space during his teens – we're not talking only about his sexuality here, but also the deep, meaningful relationships he'll form, some of which will last a lifetime. Your son is now in an intense phase of **learning about intimacy** and relationships. For the first time, his relationships have become eroticised, and he is discovering how to deal with new urges and drives within a romantic relationship.

Attachment is something he is re-learning to negotiate. Interest in the female body is at an all-time high. As he is maturing, his male friendships take on new meaning for him. This can also be an intense phase of establishing who his real friends are, and he needs to understand how to be a true friend himself. Team sports help with this process, as it encourages loyalty and camaraderie. Alcohol, drugs and parties are a part of the choices he has to make, and strict boundaries need to be in place so that a boy does not compromise his maturing conscience.

As his relationships become more intimate, your son will experience feelings of real betrayal, of being let down and being disappointed by friends. He feels it at a deeper level because his friendships with his close friends have become much more important now – his feelings have begun to deepen, so there's a much more intense connection.

You may find that he does not want to talk about intimacy. Why not? Because this is all so new to him. He's embarrassed. He doesn't know what he's feeling and is fragile. Never joke about this topic. You should already have talked to him about sex by the time he is sixteen; it is much easier to have that conversation when he's thirteen or fourteen. He needs to know that you are available to speak to. And remember that you have a role to play, as you are the standard by which he will measure every girl or woman he meets.
- Friendships become all-important. Acknowledge that your son's generation values friendship and relationships far more than ours did.

- Never stop telling your son that you love him (this is especially true for his dad!).
- Ask your son for (and listen to) his opinion. Our boys have incredible insight regarding issues of, among other things, morality, politics and relationships. They understand the complexities of the 'big issues' and want to discuss them. Your son needs to know that you value his views and that his opinion counts.
- Show an interest in what your son does, but accept that he will not tell you everything; secrets are part of being a teenager.
- It is not a good idea for him to form a strong, intimate relationship with a girl that lasts for more than six months in which he becomes more and more isolated from the family when he is only fifteen or sixteen. He should not be completely engrossed in one relationship during this phase, when there are so many other skills that he still needs to develop. It is better for him to be going out and mixing in groups.

THE HERO'S JOURNEY

On a deeper level, we could call these teen years 'the hero's journey'. Comparative mythologist Joseph Campbell famously wrote in his book *The Hero with a Thousand Faces* (1949) that almost all cultures have rites of passage that mark our transitional phases.

The teen years are a tumultuous phase that transitions a boy into man. To make it to adulthood on both an emotional and spiritual level, certain steps and risks need to be taken to 'hone' the body, mind and soul. In many stories and fables (for example, *The Lord of the Rings*), the hero goes through a phase of powerlessness or faces possible failure. In this period, his task may feel impossible, and he may feel stuck or overwhelmed. It is as if he is in one of those dreams where we keep trying to run, but can't get away from the villain, or our feet are stuck and we can't move. Sometimes his teen years can feel this way for a boy. Just when he feels grown up, he is reminded of his dependence on others or his inability to perform. This sense of 'loss of control' brings up immense feelings of vulnerability. To a teen boy, this translates as weakness or being less of a man.

The teen boy has to dig deep to access his personal power and sense of self, and even deeper to discover his dignity and strength. Yet, in the hero's journey, the release arrives when he faces his fears and recognises that that which may appear to be a weakness is, in fact, a strength.

My son walked the hero's journey too. He is a redhead and was teased relentlessly as a teen. This wounded him deeply, yet he also developed a wicked sense of humour and an honesty about it that was disarming. It was only in his twenties that red hair became fashionable. I think he is still surprised by the extra attention he gets because of his wavy red looks and great sense of humour.

To become a man, a boy needs to seize permission to live his own reality. The hero begins his journey by not knowing who he is, unaware of his capacity or talent, without intention or abiding life principles. Along the way, he meets those who can lead or teach him; he learns to trust his gut, he is let down but rises back up again and finds his path. If he is deeply wounded or betrayed, it is this very wound that guides his journey. He is always searching for affirmation and approval, since he always feels that he is not enough. He will be set tasks and tests to accomplish, but he needs to prevail because he has a vision or a sense of a better way or a safe place. Helpers and markers will show him the truth or the way, but there will always be something within him that will whisper to him … and it is to this deep inner voice that he must listen, as it will give him the strength to say 'no' to others' ideas of the path that he should take.

For some time, though, he may succumb to what others tell him to do or who to be. It takes a lot of courage for a boy to stand up to a strong dad, for instance. For years, he may act out roles and stereotypes. He may sometimes be alone and sometimes with many, but eventually he will find his core values and his destiny, purpose and essence.

The goal is to integrate all that he has learnt, and to move to the beat of his own drum. This is the hero's journey, as it is the teen's journey. And if we embrace this myth, it becomes clear to us as parents that our sons have their very own soul journey, and every success and struggle will be an opportunity for him to discover who he is and who he wants to be within his community.

It is our role to curiously participate, not to control or direct. We should not deprive him of what he can learn by trying to save him from his struggles. We should raise him to become who he is supposed to be, and understand that his life belongs to him and is not a project for us to manage. The hero's journey is a process of becoming and a natural movement towards wholeness.

MORALITY FOR BOYS

What is your son's definition of morality? This can be tricky question for him, so have a discussion: what are his views on pornography, smoking, drinking, bunking school and stealing? Discussions around values and morality are very important; you have to be his role model, but we need dialogue in these areas, too.

You may feel that you spend your life telling your fifteen- or sixteen-year-old about consequences. This is because the internal conscience isn't fully developed yet. Developing empathy and concern for others will lead your son to acquire his own values and morality, which, believe it or not, already began at about age five or six, when he made his first best friend. The stages are all being repeated at higher and riskier levels – now there are graver consequences than during those early days.

Morality starts with a fear of punishment. It can remain at an immature level (for example, you might hear men bragging about how they got away with something bad they had done, which indicates that they have very little internal morality). Morality begins to be internalised at around age sixteen, and a conscience starts to form. Conscience deepens when a person starts recognising that their negative intention can have a bad effect on the people around them.

So, although morality can grow ever deeper, it certainly starts with a fear of being punished. But, if we only focus on external punishment with our teenagers, their internal morality won't begin to develop as it should. Let's look at how you can help to develop your son's conscience with these practical tips:

- Start looking for opportunities to air your opinions, right or wrong, and your core values. For example, let's say that you've read something that you feel outraged about and you discuss it at home. Your son might yawn at the table when you talk about corruption or fraud, but don't let that put you off: discuss why you see this as a bad or a wrong thing. And don't shy away from the tough subjects: discuss rape versus consensual sex and its impact, for instance.
- Praise good acts. You want to help him begin to develop the muscle to really reflect on right or wrong and good or bad. Talk about others' amazing acts of kindness, and praise him when he speaks kindly to a sibling, or when he is being helpful, generous, honest, etc.

- Praise and name things. Normally we don't say, 'That was a considerate act.' We just say, 'That was nice.' We have to apply our minds a little and name those things that we see as steps towards a good conscience, so that he can start internalising them as his own standards.
- Do you trust yourself and your son? Do you demonstrate friendship skills? Know your own values, beliefs, etc. and discuss these, and tell your own moral stories. Improve your own relationship skills. Talk to him about girls and about your own experiences as a teen.
- Be as non-judgemental as you can.
- Be careful regarding privacy issues. It's all right for him to keep some information private.

HOW TO ENCOURAGE EXPLORATION

This is a hard one for some of us: it means that you are going to give your son a whole lot more freedom than he had as a pre-teen, within safe parameters, and that there will be consequences for his actions. But how can you encourage this exploration, which is a necessary step for the teen boy to reach adulthood?

Give him more freedom

When your son goes out, he will have to make his own decisions, and you'll have to deal with any wrong choices as they happen. However, always let him know that you trust him and that you believe he has it in him to make the right decisions. Often, exactly what you fear will happen: he is going to disappoint you, and he is going to let you down. Perhaps you'll gate or ground him, but once the consequences for a bad decision have passed, you need to say, 'Now we'll try again.'

You can't stop the exploration process, because he's going to explore anyway. You can delay the exploration, but it's best for everyone if the process is allowed to start gradually when he is thirteen or fourteen. By the time he is sixteen, he will have some experience in making decisions and will know that, while there are consequences for making bad ones, you trust him to get to the right one (eventually).

Let him test boundaries

This is the stage of boundary testing. Where before he saw himself in terms of a collective identity – one of the family – he is now moving towards his own identity. In forming his own identity by discovering what is important to him, he is, in effect, setting his own boundaries. This can happen metaphorically or literally, for example, when he locks his bedroom door. This is an important step in self-care, and it will help him to keep himself safe and indicate what he will or won't be responsible for. If you allow your son to say no to things sometimes, it will build his confidence and enable him to develop good mental and emotional tools. He will, however, need to take responsibility for the consequences of his own boundary setting.

Help him be realistic

There is often tension between the ideal self and the actual self, and it can get teenagers into trouble. Maybe he's uncoordinated but wishes he was a rugby star; maybe he's quiet and shy but dreams of holding the floor with ten girlfriends hanging on his every word ... If your son can never meet the demands of the ideal self, depression can follow.

So, help your son plot a realistic progression towards realistic goals: ask 'What are the steps towards what you want to achieve?'; then 'What do you need to take that first step?' If he hates running and is not prepared to practise kicking or throwing the rugby ball every spare moment until he overcomes his lack of coordination, how on earth is he going to be a rugby star? Would achieving a different goal that involves something he loves still give him the confidence he sees in that 'ideal self'?

If he's uncoordinated but really wants to be part of the sports scene, what about becoming a junior referee, or an assistant medic? Does a team sport feel like the right the way to go, or would excelling at an individual sport align better with his nature? Is he comfortable with the school-sports set-up, or should he rather try a pursuit like rock-climbing, where he'd meet an entirely new group of people?

So, what are your son's talents and passions (beware, they are not always the same thing, and they may not be what you think they are)?

We need to support teens and give them the opportunity to explore their identity where they can, because without exploration they will not reach a defined decision about what their identity is, or be able to commit to it. Exploration and the discovery of self go hand in hand.

Parenting tip from the therapist's couch

Moms have all heard about the necessity to #letgo of boys so that they can explore their independence and achieve autonomy. These are two vital aspects of teen development. It sounds good logically, but the emotional impact of a boy pushing you away or 'doing his own thing', without you, hits hard. One day you are the best mom and he wants to marry you, and the next thing it's 'Chill, Mom!', and the feeling of rejection descends upon us. Most mothers react either by trying harder to please or by lurking on the periphery and focusing a telescope on him. It's a recipe for disaster!

The best advice I can give is to start with yourself. FEEL and own your feelings. Being rejected or dismissed by someone we love is horrid. It hurts. Next up: UNDERSTAND the process. A teen needs to feel in charge of his life. The good news is that if he does start pursuing something because *he* wants to (and not because Mom says he must), he becomes motivated. And this is essential. And, of course, it's time for you to get a life!

You need to allow your teen to have his own experiences, and then to feel how this affects you, and why. In that way, there is growth for both of you.

Ask Megan

Question: 'My son only does what he wants to do, and in his own time. It seems my rules are not his rules! He is always challenging any rule I give him, and wants to negotiate it.'

Answer: 'One of the most frustrating things for parents is that adolescents will not follow reasonable instructions, or meet deadlines. We all know the adolescent mantra: "You are not the boss of me!" One of the teenage tasks is to discover autonomy, and this is a hard-wired inclination to do things their own way. Maybe this will help you. There are three vital tasks: 1. SHOW UP; 2. GROW UP; 3. WAKE UP. He needs to mature and develop his skills. And he must discover his soul's unique calling. You can encourage the first and coach the second, but only he can complete the third, on his own.'

THE FOUR TYPES OF BOYS AND HOW THEY RESPOND

Author Gretchen Rubin named the 'four tendencies', which we all have when responding to expectations, in her book *The Four Tendencies*. I explain each one below. Can you see your son in any of them? Or yourself? I'm not a believer in hard and fast rules about personality types, but Rubin's ideas are useful, since they will help you understand how your teen responds to an instruction.

1. The Upholder

This personality type is motivated by fulfilment, and often responds readily to inner and outer expectations. This could be his own expectations versus others' expectations of him. They are high achievers and will do things upon instruction. Their inner motivation and your expectations align easily. So, they will do what's good for them. They like to tick things off from a list. They say things like, 'I like schedules and rules, yet I'm happy to draw them up on my own.' Parents delight in these teens, but often fret that they are 'working too hard'.

2. The Questioner

This type wants information *and* must meet his own inner expectations. If you are telling a questioner to do something, their response is normally, 'Why?' As a parent, you can help this teen make sense on a personal level. Give him the reasons and let him customise the rules or chores. Encourage him to research the best options. If he understands an instruction, he will do it.

3. The Obliger

These are the people-pleasers and therefore meet outer expectations first. They want support, validation and like to do something in a group. Parents should encourage these teens to sign up to group activities. They are motivated by their peer group and struggle to meet the expectations they impose on themselves. They say things like, 'Please monitor me. Help me stick to it, please.' These teens need you to be around to assist them.

4. The Rebel

If your teen is a natural rebel, then the teen years are tricky! They resist their own inner expectations *and* those of others. They say things like, 'I will do it in my own time. I choose. No one tells me what to do.' They love freedom of choice, and you can't lock them in. Rebels love the act of resisting the norm, and parents need to keep reminding these teens of possible outcomes. As a parent, you need to learn to frame an instruction in a rebel way: 'Here are the options and here are the consequences. You choose, as I think that you know what you want.' Present them with both options and consequences.

> *Worksheet: Homework*
> Think of some practical examples from your son's life where he demonstrates the following developmental tasks in your home:
> - **Autonomy.** He needs to feel that he has some control over his life. How do you react to this? How do you parent it? In what way can you adapt and aid his need for autonomy?
> - **Identity**. He needs to develop a clear idea of who he is, which involves an understanding of his strengths, weaknesses, values and beliefs. How do you react when he is trying to explore his identity through fashion, hair, music or activities? How can you parent this in a way that makes room for his growth? Where do you clash?
> - **Morality**. He needs to explore what is right from what is wrong and examine values and beliefs, and discover his own conscience. How do you encourage this? What clashes do you have with his newfound value system?
> - **Intimacy**. He needs to learn relationship skills and the thrills and spills of love outside the family. How are you reacting to his need to be close to friends or girls? Are you over- or under-involved? How do you parent his new impulse for intimacy? Can you find a way to parent this that allows him some freedoms? What are the clashes?

CHAPTER 7

Crippling parenting mistakes you may be making

'No matter how great a parent you've been, at some point your teenager will pull away from you. The good news is that this is totally natural.'

– Lisa Firestone, *Conquer Your Critical Inner Voice*, 2002

The inner critic, or that judgemental voice in your head, is deeply entrenched by adulthood. It prompts our reactions. Your son is busy internalising the voices of his parents and other influential figures like house masters and seniors.

Therefore, the more we criticise or put him down (you're lazy, it's bad, that's mean, that's wrong), the more negative his perception of himself becomes, just as he is turning into his own internal judge. However, the more we nurture and affirm the things we like about him, and the more we remind him of what we would prefer to see him do, the more opportunity he has to evolve his compassionate inner voice.

MISTAKES THAT CAN DERAIL THE PARENTING JOURNEY

Let's take a closer look at some of the parenting mistakes that can turn the teenage years into a hardship for all, and what you can ultimately do to make it easier on everyone.

You are being ruled by a millennial

Many modern parents, both dads and moms, allow their teens to rule the home. After dealing with thousands of parents, I'm always amazed at how strong adult figures become submissive, passive or confused around their teens. Many of this generation of adolescents (millennials) are assertive, outspoken and bright, with good boundaries.

Most of you are Generation X parents, who run child-centred homes that are great for toddler development, but not so much for teens. Teens need adults to provide them with structure and to guide them. Many parents are scared to parent for fear of 'squashing' their teen's individuality and creative impulses. We forget that we are the ones who have the neurological circuits that rely on the prefrontal cortex, while teens rely on the cerebellum and hindbrain. Adults are therefore far better than teens at deductive reasoning and a holistic vision, and we understand the impact of consequences. Teens, on the other hand, are impulsive, emotionally charged, and love short-term, instant experiences.

So, this is a reminder to be the adult. Use your hard-earned reasoning ability and stand your ground regarding good values, such as caring, sharing, perseverance, responsibility and making healthy choices. You may at times feel that you are lagging behind your savvy teen, but you are streaks ahead on experience and sound reasoning.

> **REMEMBER:** Being an adult is first and foremost being comfortable in your own skin and not pontificating on a soapbox.

You are totally overparenting

Most of us are still trying to parent our sons the way we parented them when they were little boys, and this lies at the heart of many of the difficulties we run into as moms of teenagers.

Let me explain. When your son was a little boy, it was very clear what you, as his mother, needed to do: pack his school bag, buy his clothes, sort out lunches, check the homework (sometimes do the homework!), organise visits to the dentist and doctor, take him to extra lessons … There were lists on top of lists of things you had to do. And how did the endless chores make you feel? Exhausted, yes, but also *wanted* – you had a sense that these were the things you needed to do and you got them done, and you felt that you were achieving things as a mother.

How to mother was clear: he needed and asked for your listening ear, your encouragement, your hugs, your involvement, your help and your time. But that all changes in the teen years.

There's a children's story about a mother bunny and a baby bunny. The baby bunny was shy and fearful of trying new things, and scared to be on his own. Mother Bunny said: 'Don't be scared, little Bunny Boy. I'll always be there for you. If you are hopping next to a cliff edge, I'll come as fast as the wind and pick you up and carry you to safety. If you fall into a dam, I'll come as a river and lift you up and place you on land again. If a hungry fox comes, I'll transform into a giant bunny and squash that fox. Never fear, Bunny Boy, Mommy will always be there for you!'

This is the grand idea of mothers – to be the great protector and a constant presence for their children. But it is the epitome of every teen boy's nightmare: Mom popping up and swooping in every time he gets into trouble.

When boys reach high school, there is a definite shift in their mindset. Not only does the school ask you to let go, his dad does too, and so does your son. Your son might even have told you to 'Get a life!' when you thought you were being a good mom by following up on all his school commitments. Think about those words. He means: 'This is *my* life. Focus on your own, and not so much on mine.' And, you know what? He's right. It's actually good advice, even if it hurts.

What is happening is that the role he needs you to play has changed. Your child starts saying, 'No, you don't understand. I am not a child. I can do this. Don't treat me like a baby.' Dads may get this before we do, and may begin saying things like, 'You are mollycoddling him. Leave him!'

Suddenly we are not being asked to do chores, even though we *want* to do them, because it gives us a sense of being part of what's happening in our sons' lives.

It is easier for us to hang onto the familiar, especially 'prep-school' parenting, since it worked before and that is what we know. A mother naturally moves in the direction of her child. But teens are naturally moving away. So we do more, trip over ourselves to please and pamper, in the hope that the golden boy will arise again; or we become controlling and rule-driven in an attempt to overcome the uncertainties.

Yet, raising this generation of teen boys requires a paradigm shift in our mothering style. Your son's energy is now focused on his friends and other interests. Maybe he is growing closer to his father. His energy is not focused on his relationship with his mom. We start realising that we are not quite as needed as we once were. We start feeling redundant. Even rejected. And how do human beings react to rejection? Not very well. We overreact, we ask more questions, we move faster, we try to do more, or we start blaming ourselves. We never think, 'Oh wait, I actually need to do *less*.' We don't say, 'When you are ready to come to me, you come to me.'

You are holding on way too tight

My oldest son was leaving at age eighteen for his gap year in Germany. My younger son turned to me and said, 'Now don't go holding on to *my* ankle.'

It was such a powerfully clear statement – one of those tough-love declarations. I could not mistake his meaning. I was already moving in closer – and he recognised it and called me on it instantly. I had to face that in myself.

We might have known that the teen years would be hard, but what most mothers do not expect is the **deep feeling of loss** that they experience at this time: the loss of the golden boy of eight, nine or ten years old who was consumed by his love for his mother, and she for him.

Now, quite suddenly, you hear a different sort of voice when you enthusiastically ask about his day: 'Chill, Mom. Get a life!' You are told to stand back. The message is clear: 'I'm not in the mood to share with you,' or 'I want to handle this myself.' It makes sense to us intellectually, and yet it ravages our emotions. No wonder the Native American tradition was to remove the boy from the mother's tepee at this age. It may seem harsh, but it allows the separating to be real and tangible, and not left in a grey area of strong emotion.

Many mothers on my courses, even mothers with seventeen-year-old boys, hadn't realised how much hurt and pain they were holding onto around the loss of their little boys, until we started talking about it. But it can be immensely comforting to realise that you are not alone and that most, if not all, of the mothers around you are mourning the same loss of control, and the loss of their little boys.

The situation can become even more complex if we perceive our son to be rejecting us. We take it personally, like a jilted lover, which can cause a strong emotional reaction.

We all react differently to what we perceive as rejection: we can experience anger and grumpiness, withdrawal, irritation or tearfulness, sadness and hurt. We are often surprised when we feel irritable and angry, and we need to pause and ask where these feelings are coming from. Normally, they are anchored in some underlying hurt, and we have to pause to recognise this.

For some mothers, it results in enormous sadness; others doubt their ability to parent this phase. And we can easily start panicking because of the uncertainty. Psychologically, uncertainty causes fear.

Unfortunately, these emotions do not help us to parent a teen. Fear can cause us to hold on to our teens too tightly, and many of us 'hold on' in strange ways. We cook more food for him, we pack more into his lunches, or we start playing his favourite rap mixes in our car in an attempt to connect to his world! Many mothers I have worked with can't identify the way they 'hold on', until I point it out.

We need to recognise the ways we hold on as a mother – for me, holding on stems from a fear of loss or feeling redundant. But we experience the loss of our sons in many different ways. For some, it can show up in obsessive and compulsive actions. I've dealt with mothers who get up in the middle of the night to repack all their kitchen cupboards, not understanding what's motivating their bizarre behaviour. In fact, it is a masking behaviour because it is too difficult to face that we are not as needed as we used to be. We simply cannot cope with how our role as a mother has changed, or the feelings this change evokes in us.

You are crushing his life force

Autonomy is when a teen boy begin to step into his own – what I call – *personal power*. The personal energy or life force that begins to awaken in a boy is a powerful thing, and he will want to start taking ownership of it.

So, what are the dangers if we do not allow him ownership of this personal life force? What if we say, 'You will only do as *I* say. It's my way or the highway. No, you can't do that. No, what a bad idea'? What are the consequences if you keep suppressing his need to take his own life force into the world in his own way?

He could rebel, or he could go 'underground', and that is another thing we fear as parents.

Let's reflect on your own teenage years. You didn't have a cellphone or a GPS, and you weren't monitored 24/7. Most of you only told your parents half of what you got up to. And half the fun of being a teenager is that your parents will never find out and never know.

Can you remember a day when you did something by yourself for the first time? You did something that was your own decision. You made a choice and took action. It could have been as simple as catching a bus, but just try to think back to when you made that decision. You might have felt scared yet empowered, and, if it went well, you felt brilliant. That was you celebrating your own life force.

One man described it to me as a powerful energy that he literally could feel rising inside of him. It felt to him as if he could conquer the world and could do anything he wanted – a kind of immortal energy. He began to make decisions for himself, for the first time, at about age fourteen. And he remembers very clearly how his parents shut it down and told him, 'That's nonsense. Don't be ridiculous. You can't do that.'

He remembers rebelling and beginning to do things for himself anyway, as an expression of his autonomy. His mother then grew very silent, cold and distant, and when he came home at night, she would get up, look at him, but say nothing.

This was so crushing for him that he felt it started a depressive phase that went on for many years and stopped him from doing what he wanted to do in life.

So, what's the lesson we can learn from this? Don't squash your teen's life force. Let him explore that feeling of having something vital to offer to the world.

You are giving credit where no credit is due

We can also do damage as a parent when we give too much praise: 'That painting is amazing' or 'That essay is just the best' or 'When you get out there, they'll know that you should be the captain of the team.'

Giving credit where no credit is due is not helpful. If you do this and they haven't earned it, they will have an unrealistic expectation of their own abilities. And then they expect that the world is just waiting for them and they don't have to do anything. You will see that your son has hero imaginings.

So, if you really don't like something he's done, tell him: 'It's not the best work you've done. I've seen so much better work from you. I think you could have improved that if you had more time.' This honest feedback allows your child to start gauging himself and prepare for the big wide (real) world out there.

Research is showing that overpraise is often linked to a 'reward and punishment' system. In other words, everything your teen does is judged as good or bad. If it's good, then we reward, and if it's bad, we punish. This creates the need for external approval. A teen is then unable to develop his own self-appraisal and self-evaluation, because he is always looking for external reward or approval. Approval becomes the only way for them to feel that they are okay as a person. So, what do we do as parents to counterbalance this?

- Remind teens that how *they* feel about *themselves* is the most important thing.
- Let your teen start making his own decisions. Let him do things his way, within limits. Trust more.
- Begin to embrace relationship-building and being present 'with' him, as opposed to dispensing right/wrong judgements.
- Give credit only where credit is due. Hold your teen responsible for his actions.
- Let him find agency. Let him have his opinion, yet be responsible for the consequences.

Worksheet: Homework

Think for a moment of one of the strongest criticisms that you have of yourself. What does that judge with the big whip in your own head say? Is it about your weight, about your thinking, about your procrastination?

And the moment you find that judgemental voice, I bet you can link it to a parent. It's either your mother, or your father, or your grandmother, or someone who was on at you as a child. It was what they said to you. Now, it has become your internal voice or critic. Ask yourself:

- Do you also have an internal voice that is kinder or softer?
- Is there also a voice that balances out the inner critic and nurtures you? Does this voice say, 'It's okay, darling, just relax. You will be fine. You're kind. I like you.'
- Do you have a kind parent voice in your head that says, 'It's okay, because tomorrow is another day and you'll get to it then'?
- Grow your nurturing voice. This is the only way to help your son develop his own self-compassion.

Parenting tips from the therapist's couch

Do you continuously **#praise** your child/teen in the hopes that you will build confidence? Or are you irritated by your teen's lack of motivation? Do you counterbalance this by telling them that they are good at everything, hoping to nudge them into action?

Another possibility is that, as supermoms, we might want superteens. So we have instilled in them the belief that they are geniuses and that they are good at whatever they do. Have we begun to develop a group of teenagers who believe that anything they want to do, they can do? Are they overestimating their talents, abilities and capacity? (It's not easy to admit this stuff, as we really do want the best for our teens.)

This tendency, linked with privilege, can result in an overindulged teen. Yikes! Sound familiar? We have wanted to keep them happy (especially in divorced or busy homes) and we have given them whatever they want, thinking that it's the best and quickest route to helping them remain happy.

This combination of giving them 'stuff' to make them happy and over-praising them has resulted in teenagers who feel entitled to the 'easy way', who believe that 'the world is waiting for them to arrive'. (Needless to say, a rude awakening awaits them as they search for their first jobs.)

Sadly, in this scenario, no value is attached to the costs and effort that have gone into the things they have. And yet we complain that our children don't appreciate things and that they are not grateful. We say, 'There are millions of starving people out there,' hoping to wake them up to reality. This does not work, because our teens have never been exposed to tough times or struggles. It is only first-hand experience that helps us to truly empathise or develop the grit we need to get through hard times. So, what can you do?

- Be aware of every time you praise or indulge your teen. Are you doing this in the hope of making life easier for yourself?
- Allow him to struggle and help your teen to work it out for himself.
- Spend time doing things together; this is more important than just giving him stuff.
- Develop a growth mentality rather than a 'praise or punish' approach. Say, 'What did you learn from that?'

You are taking the struggles away from him

A young man came to see me once due to his crushing depression. He had launched his own business straight after university, but it completely failed. He had borrowed money from his family and it was all just a disaster. He couldn't get out of bed or face the world. These were parents who just completely adored their only son, but they didn't have a realistic attitude towards him. His mom always told him how fabulous he was, and that the world was waiting for him. This was a myth he had believed for years ... So, having to deal with a competitive world was just too overwhelming for him.

Parents, stop trying to shelter your children from hardship. The time has come to put an end to this behaviour and let your child start being accountable. Allow him to start feeling the knots. Let him fight his own battles in life. *Praise effort, not outcome.* Encourage the idea of learning from his struggles and that making mistakes is worthwhile.

You cannot save your teen from himself or his own life! It's his to live, learn from and discover.

You are idealising him

There is another pattern within the mother/son dynamic that is worth mentioning: that of the mother raising her little 'prince'. Here the son is idealised as the perfect man.

Often, a son may buy into this model and act out everything that Mommy wishes: he is the best student, sportsman, son and companion for her. This boy might be in danger of developing narcissistic tendencies, where he always expects all women to see him as perfect and the 'only one'. He might expect a woman to adore him and want to do his bidding. He fails to see that in real relationships, loving someone means accepting those traits that are different from yours, as there is no such thing as the perfect person.

Exalting your son can be very damaging for his future relationships.

I was once consulted by a young man's girlfriend, who didn't know how to cope with his narcissism, as she called it. It turned out he was brought up by an emotionally needy single mother who thought that love meant allowing her son to do just as he pleased, whenever he pleased. Because of her own need to have him close, she aimed to please him constantly by doing everything for him and not expecting anything in return.

This boy grew into adolescence undisciplined and narcissistic, and as a teenager he was unable to commit to anything, and was wholly unaware of his own or others' feelings. Since he could not recognise boundaries, his own or those of others, he was often disruptive, and felt entitled to special treatment by teachers. He also blamed others for everything that did not go his way. As a partner, he was impossible, doing whatever he pleased and getting abusive if his girlfriend made reasonable demands. Many of his relationships failed and he often had illicit affairs.

It is essential that a man grows out of his adolescent tendencies and learns self-regulation, self-discipline and emotional awareness of the impact his self-centred behaviour can have on others. A mother can and should help with this in the teen years.

WHAT YOUR BOYS ARE TELLING ME (AND THAT YOU NEED TO KNOW)

I asked a few boys about their relationship with their mother now that they are in high school:

> *'High school made my relationship with my mom a bit strange because I am more independent, and sometimes she says "let's go do this" and I'll say "no", but it's not that I don't want to do it with her, but it's because I don't want to do it any more. At prep school, if my mom said "we are going here", I went with her immediately. I sort of do what I want to do, but within reason. I don't always get my way, but I always get a say in what goes on.'*

> *'My relationship with my mom has really matured. At prep school, we did discuss things, but it wasn't like full disclosure from both sides, I think. And now, because I am more mature, any topic that comes up around the table we discuss in-depth and between us, and we can tell each other anything really.'*

> *'In prep school, my mom would give me a basic description of the topic or whatever was happening somewhere. But now we can speak about anything and I can get her perspective on it.'*

> *'When I was younger and maybe in Grade 9 when guys started with alcohol, I didn't want to tell her everything because I didn't want to get my friends in trouble. I suppose I've learnt that, for her, it is not a problem what other people do. It's about me. So I can speak (but I won't snitch on my friends and give her*

a bad impression of them). I can speak about what people do in my social circle or in my grade and it's a full disclosure.'

'Your relationship with your mom changes as you go through high school and how you act and how you treat her maybe. Like when I was young, I would shout at her about something silly, but that doesn't happen any more.'

'When you are in prep school, you get treated like you are at prep school, but when you go to college, you get treated older and older. And as a boy, you treat your mom as a boy sees the world and then as you grow up, then you treat her as a man that sees the world, and so you can see the contrast between that and how it would improve.'

'I think one of the most important things here in this relationship is that my mother trusts me because my mom lives in Tanzania, and so the only times I get to see her are in the holidays. Trust is the one thing that keeps our bond together because I think of her trust and how much she supports me. If my mom didn't support me or trust me, I don't think our relationship would have been as strong as it is right now. When I give her a call and I haven't talked to her in a while and the first time I hear her voice and I tell her one of my problems, she says something like, "I know that you are independent now, so you go deal with it – I trust you. I support whatever you are going to do, but just make the right decision."'

> **Worksheet: Re-parenting the self**
>
> We are all proud of our sons, but if you're honest, on a scale of 1 to 10, how intense is your pride in your son and your awe of him?
>
> If it's right up there at 10, spend some time thinking about the effect of being mothered by a parent who is in awe of their child. Ask yourself:
> - What damage can such awe and idealisation do?
> - How do you feel about the idea of raising a narcissistic, selfish, ego-driven man?
> - Instead of placing your son on a pedestal, do you hold him accountable?
> - Do you find that you encourage or expect certain behaviours because he is a boy? What examples can you think of?
> - How does society, and your own personal belief system, support these stereotypes?
> - How does one overcome these prejudices?

CHAPTER 8

Respect the bro rules

'As little boys, we learn that being labelled tough grants you a certain type of social capital.'

– Wade Davis, *The Mask of Masculinity* (TEDxUF), 2016

My youngest son was fifteen, and I was navigating the complexities of single motherhood, my psychology practice, my friendships and, of course, dating and sex. Yes, that definitely came last. I hardly had the time to work out if the current man in my life was good, bad, sad or glad, when my son came back from sport on a Friday to settle in for the weekend with the frown and attitude of a rival male.

He cornered me in the kitchen: 'If that dick ever comes back to our house, I'm leaving and I'm not coming back!'

I was stunned, and I knew he meant it: Dad was just one suburb away, and so was boarding school. I contemplated, thought, wrote, walked and spoke to my besties. There was no doubt that my son was right. My fledgling relationship was below par, and his zen 'klap' helped me see that I was being a bit of a desperado.

SIZE MATTERS!

There is an instinctual patterning in boys and men that is as old as humanity itself. The bigger boys and men rule the pack. It is clear in evolutionary psychology, and part of the male mammalian hunter syndrome.

Pick up any men's magazine or flick through any of the gaming apps and you will find the male stereotype. Bigger is better. Whether we are aware of this or not, it is deeply instinctual. A teen boy is hyperaware of the male pecking order, and is sensitive to finding his way and fitting into the male world.

Added to all this, your son is dealing with the effects of testosterone and neurological changes that are wreaking havoc on how he feels. He is experiencing increasingly angry feelings and high excitement tendencies. Steady testosterone levels are best to contain this.

How to handle your testosterone-fuelled son

The young male has a need for structure and order. It is therefore very important for parents and teachers to establish clear boundaries and hierarchies for the boys in their care. Otherwise, if left to their own devices, scuffles, bullying and power struggles will emerge between boys as they attempt to establish their own pecking order.

In order for boys to feel safe and get on with the tasks they need to accomplish in your home, they need to know the answers to three questions:

Who is in charge?
What are the rules?
How will the rules be applied?

Research also suggests that in a home where there are unclear expectations and a lack of structure, boys feel unsafe and anxious. Insecurity and anxiety are covered up with bravado and noise, as boys run around trying to fill the space and assert themselves in an attempt to act tough and mask their feelings of vulnerability. John Gray's latest research (*Beyond Mars and Venus*, 2017) shows that men are at their calmest when they are goal-directed and solving problems. This keeps testosterone levels steady. When they only talk about their feelings, their oestrogen levels may go up, causing them to feel out of kilter and aggression may be the result.

A mother can feel overwhelmed by the level of male bullying, bragging, wrestling and shouting that goes on, and as a result may resort to being harsh, abusive or unfair. A boy's anxiety levels can then increase, and he becomes emotionally overwhelmed. It is significant that boys (and perhaps men, too) respond to emotionally charged situations with a typical fight, flight (withdrawal) or freeze response. If the situation is very aggressive, testosterone levels may spike, causing huge defensiveness.

A mother may not understand a boy's need for structure and order, and that most young males want rules and procedures that are strictly enforced in a kind, fair and consistent way.

This male leadership approach decreases their levels of anxiety, causes a drop in macho behaviour, balances out testosterone and allows them to focus on whatever task is at hand.

Clearly the influence of testosterone on behaviour cannot be denied and should make it clear that no little boy, given his genetic make-up and levels of testosterone, could ever be feminised. So there is no danger that boys will become effeminate because they play with girls or dolls or try on dresses. And yet research is showing that when a boy whines or complains a lot, it causes a spike in oestrogen, pushing him towards his feminine side.

The orientation towards action that characterises men and boys predispose them to immediate reactions. We need to help boys exercise self-regulation so that they can consider alternatives. This can be followed up by problem-solving, clear communication and empathy.

THE BRO RULES (MALE STEREOTYPING)

Gender intensification takes place during adolescence, and the teen boy's newfound macho behaviour is directed at his mother. Strong and masculine have often meant dominance, and femininity, compliance. Most often, this is instinctual and not a conscious process. Your son is naturally compelled to follow the pack and the 'rules' of being a man:

Young boys	Early/middle teens	Older teens
• Don't cry when hurt • Boys play with boys • Winning is good	• Don't talk about feelings • Don't get too close to your guy friends • Laugh when uncomfortable • It's okay to make fun of others • Sport makes you a real man	• Never show fear or uncertainty • Having sex and scoring makes you a man • Drinking is cool • Look cool at all times • Girls and women are sexy • It's a man's world • Make a name for yourself on your own • It's okay to be aggressive • Mask your real feelings, even excitement

(Adapted from Pollack & Biddulph.)

A teen boy needs his independence and autonomy. He wants to stay connected, but is trying to figure out 'his own terms'. Mom needs attachment, closeness and control. The potential drama is obvious.

Being dependent on mom means he's 'weak' (according to the male pack), so boys often flex their muscles around her in an attempt to prove their independence and maleness. The message Western society sends out on how men should be – full of machismo, virile, not showing emotion – is not what maleness is and should be.

Men traditionally flex their muscles in two ways: through dominance or hard silence. As a boy begins to grow into manhood, he tries to gain a new position with his mother. Sometimes it's via strong assertion; other times it's criticism, advice or silence. This can be unsettling for any woman!

The teen boy wants a relationship with his mother that is more equal, yet separate. He is trying to establish his masculinity, which he is still unsure of. The first step is to push against the feminine that he has clung to for so long. This is a crucial time in his development.

Mothers need to be wise and empowered during this stage, and focus on their own satisfactions in life. But, at the same time, they need to continue to love and stay connected to their son, and hold him accountable for his actions and words in order for him to be safe, strong, yet still in touch with his heart. If a mother really understood masculine development, she would allow her son to make more of his own decisions, grant him his male 'cave' time and encourage him to problem-solve, as well as look out for others. The male energy loves to be a hero on a mission, to be the protector and to solve problems.

It's fine to be proud of your son's budding maleness, but I always warn against awe, as I think a mother needs to be demanding yet not directive. Ask, request, and then let him solve things. Break the feminine stereotype of 'looking up to a man'; let your son earn your trust. Demand caring and kind behaviour, and ask him to be more engaged.

At the same time that you want your son to be responsible and accountable, you also still want control. This creates another clash. A boy can only develop these positive characteristics by becoming more independent and making choices for himself. As a parent of a teen, you aren't going to get through this stage if you continuously use an authoritarian style, or on the other hand, if you are his servant. If you are supportive and assist with the developmental tasks, you resolve any conflict and, at the same time, raise the kind of adult you want in the long term – one who can make his own decisions and self-regulates, and is considerate of others' needs.

YOUR TEEN AND HIS FRIENDS

Your son needs friends, and longs for them. They become key to his development and emotional well-being. Yet the moment you put a bunch of boys together, they act differently. They have their own language with all kinds of male 'posturing' going on.

One young man told me that he cannot explain it. He goes to hang out with his friends and talk, but the next minute there's an energy around and the need to jostle, compete or play a game. He says it just happens, and that it's something to do with how testosterone or instincts affect boys when they are together.

Every time I have walked into an all-boys dining area at a boarding school, I have certainly felt this. There's a palpable energy among a group of boys hanging out together. It's loud, it's action-orientated and it definitely has its unspoken rules.

Let's look at some of these 'bro rules' that many psychologists talking about masculinity verify.

The bro rules and friends
- Stand up for your buddies no matter what.
- Actions speak louder than words.
- Be there when your friends need you.
- Stay cool no matter what.
- Teasing is an acceptable way to show affection – just don't go too far.

Things to be concerned about
- If your son is lonely.
- If your son does not socialise.
- If your son does not bring his friends home.
- If your son does not have friends of both sexes.
- If he has a permanent girlfriend too early and they isolate themselves.

Is your home 'boy-friendly'?
- There is somewhere they can gather comfortably and have privacy.
- You have plenty of food and drinks that they like and are allowed to snack on.

- There is stuff that they like to do (pool table, music, video games).
- You know your son's friends and greet them by name.
- You don't criticise him in front of his friends.

How to encourage his friendships
- Involve his friends in some family activities.
- Get to know his friends' parents.
- Praise his acts of friendship openly.
- Tolerate the loud music and loud voices as much as you can.
- Don't constantly object to his phone usage.

Why friends of the opposite sex are important
- Boys do not feel the need to compete with girls.
- Girls offer different viewpoints and activities in social situations.
- Girls make it safe for a boy to express his feelings.
- Co-ed friendships demystify women.

Ask Megan

Question: *'My son's friend is rude, disrespectful and a bad influence. It upsets me every time he comes around and he has no manners at all. My son sees no wrong in him. How do I handle this?'*

Answer: *'We can always find a list of reasons why our son's friends are not good enough. Take your eye off the problem and turn the telescope around. Ask yourself why you are reacting so strongly. Then ask your son what it is he enjoys about this friend. The most important aspect of this situation is the communication and not inhibiting his actions. You may be surprised by your son's response: "We both like surfing. I'm helping him with his maths." Once your son has opened up, don't respond with a moralistic or defensive approach. Think about his response first. If you do have factual evidence of bad behaviour, then speak up: "I find your friend clashes with our family values. What do you think?" He might say, "Mom, you are overreacting. You don't understand him." You might reply, "Perhaps that is true. But I do know the friends we choose in life have a huge influence on who we become." Then leave it at that.'*

WHAT YOUR BOYS ARE TELLING ME (AND YOU NEED TO KNOW)

I asked a few boys where they find their friends (in or outside of school), and at what age they found a really close, best friend:

'I think it mostly happens at school because you see them every day. Because there are about 140 boys in a grade, there are so many different personalities.'

'No one should worry about trying to make friends because you will find a group that shares your interests or shares what you want to do or sees eye to eye with you.'

'You will definitely find people in school who will become friends. Just because there are so many different people that there will be a group of people who will gravitate towards each other.'

'I have nineteen best friends. It just depends.'

'You have different best friends. I have friends from when I was very little and although we have grown into different young men with different interests, we still have that bond from when we were little, but you will always have best friends along the way.'

'I found a best friend in prep school, but that can change.'

WHEN MOM BREAKS THE BRO RULES

Women are notorious for talking about their kids and their achievements, and telling other people about them. Boys just don't get that. He could have come first in maths: you tell someone, even his grandmother, and he'll think it's a disaster. You have to see it through male eyes. Boys are taught about honour, loyalty, 'the guy code', the buddy system, and what expresses all of these? The code of silence. They love it. It makes them feel heroic; it makes them feel like they are living some sort of legacy and are on a mission, so they stand by their buddies. They do not tell! Loyalty and honour are hero traits, and they are really motivating and important to teens.

Moms don't know anything about this. We are not going to be proud of the fact that we have done some secret task together and that no one knows about it. We don't get it. But it's incredibly important to a boy. We must be clear about this: as moms of boys, we don't share their information. And if we need to share their information, we have to ask their permission. Just say, 'I really want to tell Gran', or 'We need to share this good news with Dad.' If he doesn't want you to tell his father, are you going to align with your son against your husband? You have to be careful about that, too.

Mothers play a dominant role in protecting and coaching a boy's feelings and inner life. She has been the one to listen, soothe and nurture; she is the one who has acted as a buffer between her son and an angry father or disapproving teacher; she has been the 'soft touch' that is always sensitive to how her son really is. Yet she represents the feminine and dependence, and as a boy's male ego develops, he organically begins to untie himself from being 'a mommy's boy'. Some aspects of this process are inevitable; some are hurried along by peer pressure and other male role models. But I believe that the mother does hold a boy's heart, safely and securely, affording him the only unconditional love he will ever get in a patriarchal society.

If a mother is needy or uses her son for her own emotional support and nourishment, she may not let him go easily, becoming reactive in some way. This reaction can take many forms, for example, passive-aggressive behaviour, manipulation and emotional blackmail, or anger and criticism, and originates from the mother's own wounds. On the other hand, a mother may believe that she is doing her son a good service by pushing him out of the nest and insisting on his independence, forcing him to cope on his own. This can also be emotionally damaging for a boy if she misunderstands his need for a slow withdrawal from her emotional cocoon.

Michael Gurian, in his book *The Invisible Presence: How a man's relationship with his mother affects all his relationships with women* (2010), says that a teen needs to find his own mirror to look into, where he sees his own heart and not an image of his mother holding it. According to Gurian, a boy needs to struggle on his own and learn to love himself. Then he can protect and honour his vulnerable inner self. He believes that many mothers 'launder' a boy's feelings or continually buoy him up whenever he can't cope, way into his adult life, rendering him unable to self-regulate his own feelings. He then needs Mom's constant approval, encouragement and praise to get him through life.

Three important tips for women about boys (and men)
I only discovered these through my own research, and wish I had known them earlier:
1. **Men cannot think and talk at the same time.** It is absolutely impossible for them. Their brains don't have that circuitry. Men need to go off and think about things. And when they do, they literally brood in silence before they are able to talk things through. So, saying to your son, 'Go and think about it and come and let me know,' is a far better tactic than putting him on the spot. He needs to go off and think about it, and once he has, he will come back and let you know what he's decided.
2. **Generally, for men, a conversation is about solving a problem.** It's about giving facts and getting to the point. Women can have a fabulous time with their girlfriends and not have a clear purpose for the conversation. Most men don't understand that a conversation can be just for bonding and building relationships. Too much emotional sharing also raises a male's oestrogen, which can cause aggression! (This is a very general rule – moms can also be task-orientated and not like 'frivolous' conversations.)
3. **When men say something, it is their final response.** As woman, we use a discussion or conversation to make up our minds. So, when your husband or son says he wants to go and see the new James Bond movie, you may as well know that he's researched which movies are on the circuit, he's got all the facts and reviews, and he knows that this is the movie he wants to see. Often, we don't respect this as women, because we think that his first response to 'What movie do you want to see?' is as tentative as ours. We definitely haven't taken into account that he has thought through the answer. It's not that women are indecisive; we just go about making our decisions in a different, more collaborative, way. We like to connect and discuss all the options.

> ### *Worksheet: Beliefs about manhood*
> Psychologists come in for a lot of criticism when they quote 'brain science' as if it is set in stone. Neurology is a science that is uncovering new data about the brain on a daily basis. The latest research has shown that women can have a 'male brain' – a brain that is stereotypically masculine in its functioning. Equally, a man can have a 'female brain' that is dominated by language and feeling more than that of a stereotypical male brain. (Watch the fascinating BBC documentary *Secrets of the Sexes* for more on this topic.)
>
> When we focus only on the adolescent brain and how it functions, we are not taking into account the impact that hormones and the influence of family, friends and school may have on a teen's behaviour. Ask yourself the following questions to explore your beliefs about manhood:
> - What are the beliefs you hold about what it is to be male?
> - How do you prefer your son to behave among other men?
> - What 'masculine' behaviours have you encouraged?
> - Do you think the men in the household must make the important decisions?
> - If your son refers to a girl's physical attributes in a disparaging way, do you laugh along?
> - Are you often called 'too emotional' or 'over-reactive' by the males in your home?
> - How often does your son or his dad say to you, 'That was only a joke.'

Worksheet: Homework

Ask your son (best for age sixteen years and older) to answer the following questions. The lowest possible score is 21, and the highest possible score is 147.

Is your son on his way to becoming a male chauvinist?	Strongly disagree 1	Disagree 2	Slightly disagree 3	No opinion 4	Slightly agree 5	Agree 6	Strongly agree 7
A man should never admit when others hurt his feelings							
Men should be detached in emotionally charged situations							
Men should not be too quick to tell others that they care about them							
Men should have home-improvement skills							
Men should be able to fix most things around the house							
A man should know how to repair his car if it breaks down							
Homosexuals should never marry							
All homosexual bars should be closed down							
Homosexuals should never kiss in public							
Men should watch football games instead of soap operas							
A man should prefer watching action movies to reading romantic novels							
Boys should prefer to play with trucks rather than dolls							

Men should always like to have sex								
A man should not turn down sex								
A man should always be ready for sex								
The president of the US should always be a man								
Men should be the leader in any group								
A man should always be the boss								
It is important for a man to take risks, even if he might get hurt								
When the going gets tough, men should get tough								
I think a young man should try to be physically tough, even if he's not big								

(*Source*: Ronald F. Levant, *Male Role Norms Inventory*, www.fatherly.com/health-science/is-my-son-sexist)

The raw score measures how much your son believes that men should conform to traditional Western masculine norms, which include restricting the expression of emotions (questions 1 to 3), striving for self-reliance through mechanical skills (questions 4 to 6), having negative attitudes towards sexual minorities (questions 7 to 9), the avoidance of all things feminine (questions 10 to 12), placing great importance on sex (questions 13 to 15), and being tough or dominant (questions 16 to 21).

You don't want to raise a boy who is high on this scale, as it means he is more likely to harass women and harm his emotional growth. So, what to do? Use his answers as a way to have a conversation about prejudices and stereotypes to shake up his viewpoints.

CHAPTER 9

You're old school! Time to change your parenting style

'On average, most women continue to mother their teen son with the same mothering style that she used when he was a boy. This is never going to work!'

This is not the time for the 'Cool' Mom or the 'Fun' Mom. It is time for the 'Coach' Mom.

GenZs (your son) have been adored, desired and cosseted. Their self-esteem and who they are have been prized. The amount of video footage and the number of pictures taken of them records every moment of their precious lives. Some of them were raised in a 'detached', develop-as-you-want way, or where their connectivity to the family has been paramount. They are also likely to have been raised either by a single mom or a step-parent (because of the high divorce rate), and with a cellphone permanently in their hands.

They have more information at their fingertips than any other generation, and they know that black-and-white thinking is a thing of the past. They believe in truth and work/life balance, and want to do the right thing that includes the community. They are wise and questioning, and cannot be told what to do.

Raising these teens requires a paradigm shift for YOU – the overly attached Generation Xer or the detached baby boomer (if you are an older parent).

COMMON CAUSES OF FAMILY DISAGREEMENTS

In an effort to understand boys' perceptions of the conflict they experience with their parents, a colleague, Dr Jason Bantjes, spent some time talking to fifteen-year-old boys about the arguments and patterns of communication they have at home. Jason learnt that while there are considerable variations in the quality of parent–adolescent relationships, there is a large degree of commonality in the issues that affect families:

- Going out, socialising and parties.
- Schoolwork, homework and academic results.
- Parents treating them as 'babies'.
- Lack of communication.
- Untidiness.
- Media addiction.

Typical MOM responses to these issues:
nagging, lecturing, worrying, anger, capitulating, lecturing, overreacting …

Typical BOY responses to these issues:
withdrawal, irritation, passive-aggressive behaviour, criticism, friends first, anger …

A clash of agendas has huge potential for ongoing conflict and confrontation. It highlights your son's need to individuate and your need to be close. As a parent of a teen, an authoritarian manner needs to be adjusted and replaced with an authoritative approach that is firm but fair. By being supportive and assisting with the developmental tasks, conflict will be minimised. After all, this facilitates the kind of adult you would like to see: a young man who can make his own informed decisions, can self-regulate his emotions and is considerate of others' needs.

PARENT-ADOLESCENT COMMUNICATION

While discussing parent-adolescent communication with Grade 9 boys, Jason asked them to answer the following four questions. After ten years of speaking to boys across four continents, I have found these to be pretty common responses:

1. What do you wish your parents would stop doing?
   - Worrying so much.
   - Taking out their bad moods on me and blaming me when they have a bad day.
   - Expecting me to be competitive.
   - Invading my space, for example by coming into my room all the time.
   - Not respecting my privacy.
   - Fighting with each other.
   - Always telling me that I am disorganised.
   - Holding me back.
   - Holding grudges, bringing up the past and holding things against me.
   - Judging my friends.
   - Being late for things that are important to me.

2. What would you like your parents to do?
   - Listen to me.
   - Ask for my opinion.
   - Give me more of a role in making decisions about things that affect me.
   - Stop worrying.
   - Accept me for who and what I am; not expect me to be someone else.
   - Be more understanding.
   - Understand that I need my independence.
   - Allow me to just do nothing when I get the chance (which is not often).
   - Remember the names of my friends.
   - Spend more time with me and appreciate having me around.
   - Get to know me better.
   - Communicate with each other more.

3. What issues do you wish you could talk to your parents about?
   - My future after school.
   - My plans for the future.
   - My social life and social media.

- What happens when I go out.
- General stuff about me and my friends.
- My life and the things that happen to me.
- Sex.
- Relationships.
- Their jobs.

4. What do you want your parents to know?
- That I love them.
- How much pressure school is.
- How much peer pressure there is, and how much pressure is caused by social media.
- That I do care and I do try.
- That I can be responsible.
- That I am different from them and that I have different goals to them.
- That I want them to be happy.
- That my skin is thinner than they think and that sometimes the things that they say hurt.
- That I love them more than anything and I want them to stop fighting (with me and with each other).

The idea of raising a boy with the understanding that he will leave you is a difficult one to make peace with. Separation and rejection issues may arise and should be reflected upon. Our teen son will be unhooking his dependence from us as he discovers his manhood, and this can be a painful process for both mother and son. If you have deep fears around separation, abandonment or rejection, you may overreact, which can complicate this inevitable process.

WHAT'S GOING WRONG WITH THE WAY YOU PARENT?

Your life process is condensing at the time that your son's is expanding. So, no matter what you do, you are probably going to go in different directions. You want him to be less self-centred, less selfish and less under the influence of his friends. You want him to look inward and consider others. But that's *your* goal, not his.

The teenage years are when a boy is negotiating his place in the world. He struggles with his ego, his identity and the world around him in an effort to learn how to be mature. It does not happen overnight and takes time, because he is asserting himself and trying to be less dependent on Mommy and other adults in his life. Friends are now more important. Clashes will naturally increase in the home, since his views and needs often differ from yours. His needs and his determination to fit in with his friends, who become all-important in his eyes, seem selfish to us.

Let's look at his processes and needs right now:
- **Autonomy.** He needs to feel in control of his own body and space, so he says, 'I'm in control. I make my own decisions.'
- **Independence.** He wants to do his own thing in his own way, so he says, 'I like being on my own. My friends come first.'
- **Identity.** He is discovering who he is, so he says, 'I am me. I'll choose who and what I like.'
- **Intimacy.** New, deeper bonds and connections are being formed as his emotional maturity deepens, so he says, 'I am interested in girls (or boys). I want my privacy.'

And what about your needs?:
- **Attachment.** We will overreact, question and overprotect.
- **To be heard.** We will nag and lecture.
- **Control.** We will give instructions and lay down rules.
- **Family connection.** We want to do things together.

The drama is obvious. Mom needs attachment, closeness and control. A teen boy needs his independence and autonomy. You hear yourself saying things like, 'Don't talk to me like that! Watch your manners, young man! I didn't bring you up like this!' In an out-of-control moment, you may even find yourself saying, 'You remind me of your father, and this is exactly why I divorced him!'

A young teen consciously knows that he aims for more space and freedom and requires some independence from Mom, yet the real developmental phases are not within his conscious control. He is not trying to hurt his mother. But this phase is unpleasant for you. Clashes are inevitable, and feelings run deep.

During workshops I've run at schools, I've asked hundreds of moms and sons what they generally fight about, and it is obvious that underlying these everyday clashes is the fact that the mother's needs are so very different from the developmental tasks that the son is hard-wired to achieve.

The priority for us as parents must be to create the building blocks that will help us develop a parenting style and strategy that works for our teenagers and for us – one that builds rather than breaks up our relationship with them. You also want to be sure that your son is going to have the necessary skills and competencies in that moment when he's making a decision that could jeopardise his safety or health, and the safety or health of others. Is he going to make the right decision?

Underlying it all is our dearest wish and deepest worry: Will he be happy? If I were to ask, 'What are the three most important things for you as a mother?', most moms would tell me:

> *His health and safety.*
> *His happiness.*
> *His relationship with me.*

A good, positive, connected relationship is the foundation he needs to build a safe, happy life. Building relationship skills with your son will carry him not only into his later teenage years, when his brain is more capable of abstract thinking and able to reason and think of consequences, but out into the world, too. By age eighteen, he will have a much better grasp of abstract thinking. Until then, you are providing that part for him – you are forever on about consequences and reminding him to remember things. But by the dawn of the teenage years, you should be finished instilling duties, tasks and rules – these are behaviours that you laid down in his childhood.

If you are still going on about this, you need to stop. If it's going to help you lessen your own anxiety, then sit down with him, make eye contact and have a serious conversation:

> *I am not prep-school mother any more. I am not asking you any more whether you've washed behind your ears or brushed your teeth. I trust that you have done that for twelve years non-stop and that it has stuck in your brain and in your heart. I am also not going to nag every five seconds about your manners and whether you have packed your bag. I want you to start getting on with that. I will check in regarding your responsibilities, but you have control of the other stuff now. Let's give this a go.*

When a mother is stuck in old mothering habits, she normally resorts to what worked in the past. Her movement is towards her son. She wants to continue to nurture and be involved by doing. Sure, there are different styles of mothering and there is a myriad of core intentions that mothers bring to their relationship with their sons. At one extreme, there is the symbiotic mother who cannot see her son as a separate being; at the other, there is the resentful mother who blames her son for her unfulfilled life and her inability to achieve her own goals.

Rather get to know yourself as a parent and as a woman and progress to senior-school mothering, which involves coaching and guiding. It is the new hat you are putting on. Your parenting should now focus on helping your son to acquire the life skills that will help him to be safe in all circumstances, and that will ensure he has the tools, capacity and competence to make the right decisions when it counts. We also want to make sure that our boy somehow is happy in his own skin. If we could tick all those boxes, we would probably sleep reasonably well – though we would always find something to worry about!

THE OTHER PARENT

A positive relationship and the ability to work together with the other parent are crucial for parenting any child. Not only does consistency between the parents help a child learn, but lack of consistency undermines a child's feeling of security. This can only worsen as the child enters adolescence. If the teen is able to divide and conquer, or, worse, cause conflict between the parents, you have a real problem. In saying this, however, if parents have different parenting styles and they accept and acknowledge the differences, then a child adapts. Differences are fine if there is consistency and acceptance.

Every now and then, a small secret between the two of you is fine. But if it's a constant 'Don't tell Dad', you need to find out why, and help them both through this.

If your son says, 'Dad is just going to mock me or put me down,' then you need to say, 'Okay, how can we change that? *I* won't tell Dad, but I would like *you* to tell Dad. How can you learn to share things with your father? What needs to happen?'

A mother aligning with her son in keeping things secret from his dad is fostering division with the father; it is a negative, when your son needs positive role-modelling to form his own positive partnerships. Secrets should not be encouraged in a home, and alliances have no place there either. These are also dangerous for your marriage. Your son's testosterone levels are raging, his brain is on high alert, and his sporting prowess and energy levels are peaking; your husband's, on the other hand, are decreasing. In fact, he could easily be going through a bit of a midlife crisis. If he sees you conspiring with his son against him, it can cause a great deal of pain – even panic. A panicking man often defends himself with anger or becomes competitive. The consequence is conflict in your marriage, and as a result all the relationships in the home will start breaking down. Instead, try to be sensitive in how you handle these different developmental stages.

And, speaking of husbands, remember that they've also been socialised to act a certain way. Many have not been taught how to nurture or be empathetic. It is important to have a private conversation with your husband and highlight that his role as a male nurturer will become more and more important during your son's teens. Your son will have questions around his own sexuality/masculinity, and it is important that these answers come from his dad. So, as his parents, you need to discuss in advance what your family values are. Leave your husband with the question, 'What do you think constitutes a good man, and how can our son begin to be one?' Don't put your husband on the spot; let him go off and think about it.

CAVEAT: In same-sex homes (where sons have two mothers or two fathers), have an open dialogue about masculinity and what it means to be a man. Discuss family roles, values and reciprocity in the home.

Worksheet: Your parenting partner

Use this worksheet to rate your different styles across seven important parenting areas. It offers an opportunity to talk about differences.

Supportive

Very						Undermining
1	2	3	4	5	6	7

Closeness to family

Intimate						Isolated
1	2	3	4	5	6	7

Emotional support

Supportive						Uninvolved
1	2	3	4	5	6	7

Time together

Frequent						None
1	2	3	4	5	6	7

Communication

Good						None
1	2	3	4	5	6	7

Sharing of chores

Equal						None
1	2	3	4	5	6	7

Ability to co-parent

On same page						Different approaches
1	2	3	4	5	6	7

Worksheet: Homework

Use this worksheet to explore the relationship with your own parents and your parented past. Place an X over the number that corresponds to how you felt about your parents during adolescence, and circle the number for how you rate your present family. Ask your partner to do it too.

Closeness

Very close							Not at all
1	2	3	4	5	6		7

Honesty

Complete openness							No communication
1	2	3	4	5	6		7

Emotional support

Supportive							Uninvolved
1	2	3	4	5	6		7

Financial support

When necessary							None/Dependent
1	2	3	4	5	6		7

Contact frequency

Comfortable							None/Too much
1	2	3	4	5	6		7

Approval

Unconditional acceptance							Critical
1	2	3	4	5	6		7

Approach to discipline

Fair							Harsh/Overly lenient
1	2	3	4	5	6		7

Other aspect of parenting

Poor							Not exhausted
1	2	3	4	5	6		7

PART 2

*'There is some wildness in us,
calling us to live everything.'*

– John O' Donohue

CHAPTER 10

Handling anger (his and yours)

*'Too many teens are becoming desensitised to violence,
and have learnt that anger is the prime way to solve a problem.
Violence is learnt, but so is calmness!'*

Here you are now – the mother of a teenage son – and I must warn you that during this period of high-firing testosterone, your son is going to drive you mad. Aggressive masculinity or hypermasculinity could show up as swearing or shouting, slamming doors or hitting his brother too hard. He may also exhibit signs of selfishness, a lack of communication, stubbornness, defiance, criticism, jealousy, blaming …

When these behaviours emerge, you can become very anxious, especially women who have experienced the masculine as a negative. The feminine side of us is fearful of aggressive masculinity, though some of us will stand up to it and fight. However, our hearts will be pounding and we'll feel fearful on the inside. So, when your son displays hypermasculine behaviour, it is going to affect you.

Does that mean that you should ignore it? The answer is no. It is wrong that he shouts at you, but at the same time, you don't need to react in a violent way as well. When he shouts at you for the first time (and it will happen!), and you find you have a very strong response, be aware of why that is. It could be that his behaviour is triggering a memory or a reaction to a past experience in you. If you ever experienced an abusive or dominant man in your life, you will be oversensitive to this type of behaviour.

Remember that your son's hypermasculinity will mirror what he is seeing around him, spurred on by the high levels of testosterone in his body. Although you should never approve of this behaviour, it does not make him a bad person. We need to moderate his behaviour by establishing firm and fair boundaries, and watching out for toxic habits. And be careful of shaming his attempts at assertiveness.

WHY YOUR SON IS GOING TO PUSH ALL YOUR BUTTONS

We all have our own 'rules' about how we like to live, as well as conditioned beliefs about certain behaviours. These rules allow you to jump to conclusions or result in rigid perceptions about your son's behaviour and its consequences.

It's important to acknowledge that you almost always have an 'agenda' when dealing with your son, and that when your agenda is challenged, you get angry. So, what agenda do you bring to a conversation?:

- Your current mood, stressors and distractions.
- Your past experiences, especially around men.
- Your expectations (who should be doing what and when).
- How you cope with emotions and self-regulate them.
- Your general assumptions and fears.

You might have the best intentions, but they get thwarted by your agenda and how you react, and by your son's agenda and his reaction. You 'miss' each other in the process.

A reminder of a few classic conclusions:

He is doing this to irritate me.
His friend/father/brother is a bad influence.
What will others think of me/us?
He should know better.
If I give in now, he'll run amok.
He is going to be another misogynist.

WHAT (THE VILLAGE) MOMS SAY

In 2018, Vanessa Raphaely and I launched a Facebook group called The Village. It is a place where parents of teens can ask for advice, share, vent and help each other. It grew so fast (30 000 people within a year) that I could not keep up, and Vanessa tackled it almost full-time, building it into an incredible community of support. Many mothers shared their views with me and, with their permission, I share some of them in this chapter:

'When my teen boys (they're twins!) hit age fourteen, I was shocked by how they suddenly changed into aggressive and dismissive little monsters. I was hurt and angry. I remained hurt and angry throughout the entire teen rejection phase – you know, the range of ways that our teens tell us to get lost (while continuing to demand our unconditionally loving presence in the form of food and shelter, and endless lifting to and from their lives outside the home'.)

'After many hours on the therapist's couch, I realised that the strong feelings I was having were similar to the ones I had when my own parents were aggressive and dismissive. I realised how much I'd been enjoying a relationship with my children that seemed to promise never-ending closeness. I realised that I feared that I would be left alone again as I was when I didn't "get on" with my own parents, or when my mom was just too busy with trying to manage things to give me the attention I desperately needed.'

'After a lot of therapy, one of my teens said, "Mom, I think we're doing better now. You're less angry, but I guess I'm also less confrontational." But, phew, what a hard couple of years to get to this conversation!

WHY TEENS GET ANGRY

Teens do tend to overreact, as they are highly stimulated and emotional. As humans, anger is often our default emotion, and also our top 'survival' emotion. It has kept us safe since the days we were hunter-gatherers, yet I have also found it to be used as a powerful male defence, while another emotion lurks beneath the surface (sometimes fear or hurt).

Our 'survival' emotions are primarily anger, panic and fear, which play a major role in alerting us to danger and keeping us safe. These emotions often trigger the autonomic nervous system, which then takes over in a powerful way and enables us to perform heroic tasks for our survival. But it is the more subtle or mixed or layered emotions that confuse us. These are difficult to unravel, and our confusion causes vulnerability and, as a result, denial or avoidance.

In Chapter 5, I explained that the teenage brain is actually not fully formed or fully functional yet, with the result that teens lack in self-awareness and self-regulation. To be able to be self-aware and intentional is only possible once brain activity is fully functional in the prefrontal cortex. Your teen is unable *yet* to use his emotional sensors to calm himself.

A teen boy can, however, be assisted by an emotionally savvy mom who speaks her feelings directly and clearly, and who can empathise with his stage of life. The mindfulness exercises at the end of this chapter will help you reach your own inner calm to better deal with your son's anger.

THE LONG-TERM VIEW: WHAT SORT OF MAN DO YOU WANT YOUR SON TO GROW UP TO BE?

Look to the future. If your son walks in at age twenty-five, what are some of the things you'd want to see? Confidence, humility, compassion, focus, conscientiousness, respect, self-esteem, sense of self, honesty, good value system, good work ethic, resilience … Is that about right?

A lot of the time a mother's list of what she would really like to see in her son will centre on relationship-orientated character traits – things he'd need to have in order to form good relationships.

When fathers write the same list, they include the following: successful, good work ethic, confident, strong, honourable, good career, good provider, intelligent. They are more concerned about status in the community and achievement in the world.

Let's rattle off some of the negative aspects sometimes associated with masculinity: self-centred, non-communicative, domineering, aggressive, addictive, risk-taking, belittling, arrogant, macho, monosyllabic, low emotional IQ, quick to anger, controlling, opinionated, irritable, violent … These are characteristics you don't want to see in your twenty-five-year-old son. Would you feel a failure if he exhibited these traits?

It is important for us as women to recognise that we have been exposed to negative masculinity in our lives, whether it was from a brother, a friend, a lover, our father or our boss. We need to understand that our responses are often not just a mother's reaction to her son; it is also because of past experiences.

We are influenced by our culture, our socialisation and our upbringing. And we are women living in what is still a patriarchal society. At some point, many of us were put down, belittled, dominated or even abused – mostly by men.

Whether we like it or not, there are still parameters around what boys should be doing and what girls should be doing. Good girls are still being raised to be compliant and pleasing, as opposed to being raucous or loud.

As a mother, we need to take into account that we are also women raising a boy and that we, too, have been socialised in terms of our attitudes, our ideas and our fears. Patriarchy in society, religion, the media and our culture has had an effect on us, just as it is having an effect on our boys. Fathers or positive male role models can, however, help boys to develop good values and attitudes. Where possible, garner help from nurturing adult males who believe in emotional literacy.

But how can we temper patriarchy and help our boys to develop good character traits? First off, change your thinking from 'boys will be boys' to 'how can I support my son to improve his impulse control?'. Promote the behaviour and positive traits (empathy, expressing feelings, contributing, self-development, kindness) that you would like to see in your son, and do it in an understanding and non-rigid way. Deal with the negative traits in a considered way. Try to put aside your reactive impulses, and come from a place that's a bit calmer when standing your ground.

Yes, you might be making a bit more allowance for his negative masculinity, but he will be held accountable for the impact it has. Why are you making this allowance? Because this stage is not going to last forever. Because he needs to connect actions with their impact. So, draw your line, but continue to calmly make him aware of the quality of presence that you bring. Keep promoting the positive without reacting too strongly to the negative; focus on the behaviour, not the person behind it.

> **Ask Megan**
>
> **Question:** *'My teenager is selfish. How do I handle this behaviour in a positive way?'*
>
> **Answer:** *'All teenagers are selfish – it is part of the teenage process to be focused on themselves. Teenagers should be given, in moderation, this opportunity to be self-focused and explore the things they like and want to do. But we need to handle these moments in a way that gets the best result. Just shouting at a teenager because they are selfish is not going to help. Next time, rather say something like, "When you always want to stay at home while we go visit Gran or have a family outing, it is really upsetting to me and to your siblings, because we miss you." Follow the pattern of: "When you ... I feel ... because ..." Don't let irritation waylay you into character assassination. Focus on the behaviour and how you feel: "I don't like it when you slam the door", not "You're an aggressive/selfish/domineering bully!"'*

BE THE ADULT IN THE ROOM

You need to move from **reacting** to **responding** to your teen.

We are all hard-wired to *think-feel-react*. From an evolutionary perspective, it was once very important to our survival to be alert to signs of danger, to think quickly and to use past experiences to prompt instant reactions. This is the flight, fight or freeze phenomenon that our nervous system manages automatically. However, in our modern lives we are not reacting to threats to our life. It is urban social life or close relationships where emotions dominate. We are often emotionally driven and emotionally volatile.

Although the quote is most often attributed to Viktor Frankl, it was more likely master psychologist Rollo May who said that 'Between stimulus and response, there could be a space. It is within this space that we can pause.' This pause offers us the opportunity to choose a healthy response. When you are experiencing really strong emotions, you can create space and pause before resorting to habitual reactions. This will enable you to go from a place of fear, anger and frustration to a place of calm.

I am not saying that you should not react at all, or do nothing. No! But you are trying to moderate a reaction that has been triggered unconsciously.

If we parent effectively and responsibly from a place of self-awareness, our parenting will not only be effective but will continue to build our relationship with our son. And the most important reason to do so is because the best way to safeguard your son against the onslaughts from outside is his relationship with you and/or anyone else in your family. It has been shown over and over that education alone does not keep our sons safe. You can teach him everything you know about drugs, brain development, alcohol, sex, HIV, but that is not going to stop him from making mistakes. The most important factor that can save your son if he's about to take a risky decision is when he weighs it up against the response from someone with whom he has a good, positive and healthy relationship. This relationship is what seems to save our boys time and again.

That is why I am suggesting that you be less reactive and more responsive (and thus, more effective) in your parenting – it strengthens the relationship and can safeguard your son against outside influences in the future.

Could your anger reaction be unconscious parenting?

Your son comes home and tells you that he's decided that he is going to switch from taking maths to maths literacy. And it's a done deal.

What happens next? You erupt! But why?

Do you start imagining his future, or do you start thinking about the past? Are you thinking: 'When my brother went from higher-grade maths to standard-grade maths, he didn't get into university. He started drinking. My son can't give up maths!' That's parenting from the past and from a place of fear.

Or are you thinking: 'What are people going to say? What am I going to tell my husband? Now all those plans we had for him to be an accountant have just fallen by the wayside. He won't get into university. My son can't give up maths!' That's parenting from the future.

Whatever the case may be, you feel a reaction. Come back to the present, and react and parent from there.

The best tactic to use in that situation is to ask your son a lot of questions, and to engage in dialogue and conversation.

There is nothing wrong with drawing on past experiences, but you need to draw on wisdom and not a fear-based assumption. Bring your experience and apply it to the present issue, but deal with your son in the present and with the current situation.

That is 'present' parenting.

SIX WAYS TO HELP YOUR SON EXPRESS HIS ANGER CONSTRUCTIVELY

Teens learn best by watching and copying, so be the person you would like your son to be. Ignite his 'mirror neurons' by acting in a way you would like him to copy.

1. Model calmness

The best way to teach teens how to deal with anger constructively is by showing them through example. Muster every ounce of calmness, use it as an instant anger-control lesson, and rather say the following:

> *I am so angry at the moment. So I am not going to speak to you right now, or I will say something I may not mean. I will calm down, think about what is best to do and we can chat later, after dinner.*

2. Exit and calm down

One of the toughest parts of parenting is when teens vent their anger towards us. If you're not careful, you'll find their anger fuelling emotions inside you that you never realised you had. Beware: Anger is contagious. Consistently reinforce the rule and rather say the following:

> *In this house we solve problems by talking them through, when we're calm and in control. I need time out. Let's talk about this later.*

3. Develop a feeling vocabulary

Many teens display anger because they simply don't know how to express their frustrations in any other way. Kicking, screaming, swearing, hitting or throwing things may be the only way they know how to show their feelings. Use the list of 'feeling' words on page 150 to rather say the following:

> *It looks like you're really angry/frustrated/irritated/insulted. Want to talk about it? You seem really irritated. Do you need to go to gym and work it off?*

4. Teach them to recognise the early warning signs

The more we help teens to recognise the physical signs when their anger is first triggered, the better they will be able to calm themselves down. Tell your teens to watch out for these obvious signs that warn us when we're getting angry:

> *I talk louder, my cheeks get flushed, I clench my fists, my heart pounds, my mouth gets dry and I breathe faster.*

5. Teach anger-control strategies

Devise physical strategies that your teen can use effectively in any situation: three deep breaths, a quick squat, clap hands three times before speaking, negotiate with yourself ('If I deal with this in an angry way, I will regret it later') ... then just walk away. Show him how to take a deep breath and ground himself:

> *As soon as you feel your body sending you a warning sign that says you're losing control, take back control by slowly taking three deep breaths from your tummy while sensing your feet on the floor.*

6. Create a calm-down image

Advise your teen to walk away, think of a peaceful place, run a lap, do push-ups, listen to loud music, hit a pillow, kick a ball, draw pictures, talk to someone, or sing a thumping rock song.

ARE YOU LIMITING YOUR TEEN'S FEELINGS?

Let's start from the position that a moody, angry teen is totally normal. As your child reaches age fourteen or fifteen, you will see the exuberant feelings shutting down. You will hear monosyllabic words like, 'I'm fine. It's cool. It's sick. It's mif.' Or even just a shoulder shrug. In response, you might have said the following:

> *Don't sit at the table with that glum face – it's affecting all of us.*
> *Buck up.*
> *You are ruining the mood by mooching around.*
> *You are depressing your sister.*

Our 'feeling' words become fewer during the teenage years, but have we stopped feelings from being expressed entirely because we are trying to stop angry feelings?

Rather try to have a bit of fun. Stick the following list on the fridge and challenge your son to use words other than 'fine'. Remember that **his brain is being rewired, and the rational, modulating centres are yet to be fully developed.** Help him develop his emotional IQ by expanding his vocabulary through this list.

List of 'feeling' words				
Happy	**Sad**	**Angry**	**Afraid**	**Excited**
Joyful	Tired	Furious	Confused	Alert
Boisterous	Hurt	Murderous	Unthankful	Concerned
Interested	Anxious	Inaccessible	Discontented	Elated
Mischievous	Frustrated	Insensitive	Inexperienced	Enthusiastic
Thankful	Guilty	Upset	Fearful	Involved
Pleased	Bewildered	Alarmed	Panicky	Stimulated
In love	Shocked	Embittered	Timid	Aroused
Believing	Cheated	Rebellious	Insecure	Busy
Naughty	Deceived	Aggressive	Tormented	Delighted
Cheerful	Hysterical	Jealous	Threatened	Elevated
Relaxed	Idiotic	Betrayed	Uneasy	Exhilarated
Happy	Apathetic	Bedevilled	Tense	Impatient
Relieved	Indifferent	Aggrieved	Appalled	Curious
Peaceful	Innocent	Irritated	Suspicious	Anxious
Friendly	Depressed	Belittled	Sceptical	Hyperactive
Confident	Burdened	Insulted	Guarded	Engaged
Patient	Lonely	Intolerant	Horrified	Intrigued
Invigorated	Desolate	Rejected	Stunned	Thrilled
Blissful	Withdrawn	Neglected	Anxious	Attentive
Carefree	Pensive	Moody	Reluctant	Energetic
Hearty	Inferior	Defensive	Impatient	Motivated
Equipped	Distressed	Vicious	Unsure	Optimistic
Refreshed	Miserable	Frustrated	Nervous	Alive
Safe	Awful	Provocative	Jittery	Jubilant
Wonderful	Sorry	Hate	Scared	Self-reliant
Calm	Cheerless	Resentful	Overwhelmed	Lively
Stable	Uncertain	Paranoiac	Intimidated	Adequate
Spirited	Disappointed	Agonised	Desperate	Daring
Romantic	Embittered	Misused	Vulnerable	Determined
Agreeable	Perplexed	Trampled upon	Horrified	Assured
Ecstatic	Negative	Unsettled	Defensive	Potent
Energetic	Mournful	Abused	Apprehensive	Assertive
Loved	Jealous	Irresponsible	Swamped	Accomplished
Optimistic	Unmotivated	Cheated	Startled	Capable
Fulfilled	Incomplete	Despised	Awed	Bold
Excited	Unloved	Provoked	Concerned	Dynamic

ENCOURAGE REVOLUTIONARY THINKING: THE MORE YOU FAIL, THE MORE YOU LEARN

We can learn positive thinking. We can learn to put a positive spin on things, and we can learn to have a broader perspective. What I like most is an approach called 'the growth mindset'. This is the idea that intelligence can be developed and is not set in stone. It is a thinking style that is touted in American education, made famous by Carol Dweck in her book *Mindset: The new psychology of success*.

The goal is to revise the dogmatic educational system of 'right and wrong' or 'pass and fail'. With this old approach, only the few achievers get any rewards. It has set up a reward/punishment system whereby learners rely on rote memory or repetition to achieve high marks, which undermines creativity and understanding of a subject. Education is now moving towards using a whole-brain approach, where the different types of intelligences are explored. Here's where the growth mentality comes in.

Dweck says that the old approach to education involved a **fixed mindset**. This all-or-nothing approach says that every child has an innate ability, and that that is the level at which the child will achieve. On the other hand, the **growth mindset** says that every child can improve by applying effort and perseverance, that the brain's abilities are 'plastic', and improves and adapts to use and circumstances.

From a practical thinking level, a growth mentality is simply asking yourself, 'What did I learn from this situation?' Failure is therefore not a problem, because it can help us learn from the experience.

Research on the growth mindset has proven that children who had been praised for their intelligence performed worse in future tasks and were fixated on comparing themselves to others. But the children who had been praised for their efforts performed better in future tasks and were more open to learning new things.

This is vital information for parents. The more we say, 'You are so clever, bright, gifted', the more we pressurise our sons into a fixed mindset. The more we discuss and dialogue about his style and strategy of performance and what he learnt or could do differently, the more our sons will be motivated to improve and discover new things. It's subtle, but it does mean that we have to give up this standard question: 'What mark did you get and where did you rank?' Rather adopt a style of quality feedback with the belief that your son can learn and improve.

If research is showing us that being fixated on marks and outcome is actually a dysfunctional thinking style, then we need to change. A growth mentality requires you to sit and reflect on what you learnt from a task and discover how to approach it differently next time. Parents and teachers can help a child realise his personal strengths and celebrate his individual accomplishments as opposed to always comparing him to a fixed benchmark.

The growth mindset suggests that making mistakes and struggling with tasks are good, as they offer us a chance to grow and stretch ourselves, and that hard work and practise are praiseworthy.

A growth mentality, positive thinking, a clear head not bogged down by negative feelings and an ability to reflect are all vital for future careers, and good for overall mental health, too.

FOCUS ON THE BODY

A relatively new field of study asks, 'What has the body got to do with our performance and intelligence?' The body, the senses and feelings are all interlinked and, of course, will directly affect the mind. The easiest way to help a boy entrapped in feelings of anger or anxiety is through his body and his senses.

We all experience the world through sensation. Sensing, or what we refer to as our five senses, are the gateways of all stimuli and information that flood our nervous system daily. As we have become visually dependent, we spend most of our days consumed with cognitive functions, so it has become essential to help a boy reconnect to his senses and his body.

Make a habit of asking your son, 'What is the sensation in your body right now? Could it be a headache, a tight chest, a sore back, a sore tummy?' I have found that boys often get sore stomachs, indicating feelings of anxiety and fear. Tension in the shoulders indicates worrying – boys seem to worry that they are not good enough and that everyone else is better than them.

In order to access feelings, be aware of sensations in the body and ask what these are telling us. But it also goes deeper than this. The more we are aware of the sensations in our bodies, the more conscious we are of being in the moment. This allows us to perceive and experience a life event, while it is happening, in a conscious way. When we develop sensory awareness, our senses become more acute; we notice more details and nuances and the uniqueness of the individual objects around us. This is a powerful resource for living in the moment and being able to experience life fully, as it happens.

In a world where we have become desensitised and disconnected because of our dependence on screens, boys cannot engage with the meaning and depth of an event. When we use our senses to connect more fully with our environment, we are establishing a warm, nourishing contact with our body, our human identity and the physical world. The body not only stores the sum of all experiences, but it is also the conduit to help release stress and trauma. (The essential field of somatic therapy is aimed at releasing trauma by using memory and sensations.)

Denying one's feelings can result in bad dreams and an unsettled unconscious. Sadly, a lot of boys think that cutting themselves off from their emotions helps them to become stronger men.

Help your son to find a balance between having feelings and being rational in situations where calm is needed.

IT ALL GOES BACK TO CONSCIOUS PARENTING

We want to be able to tap into our highest wisdom and share the best of ourselves with our family and son. I have found that conscious parenting is the best approach. But it does require you to practise being mindful: take time to pause, breathe, look inwards and find ways to calm down. Come back to the present moment, and be plugged into a fresh experience of the now.

Are you operating out of habit or with intention?

Remember Chapter 3, where we spoke about being intentional? Parenting unconsciously leads to bad habits and can undermine good relationships.

When we parent in this habitual manner, a lot of different emotions will arise, which can trigger anger, anxiety, guilt or shame. It's then easy to blame the teen for causing the problem: 'You make me feel so frustrated!' It's a vicious circle of fixed mindset, habitual behaviour, anxiety, conflict and blame. It's no wonder that the son withdraws or acts out and the parent feels anger or frustration.

So, what's another approach? Instead of blaming the 'problem' teen for causing whatever the situation may be, we instead look at ourselves. We are not blaming ourselves, but instead consider our role in the relationship. After all, we are the adults and we need to take responsibility for our own feelings and actions. It is about embarking on a path of growth and self-awareness, where we recognise the opportunity to learn about ourselves through our parenting practices. It is a conscious and more awake parenting approach that happens when a parent is centred and empowered. There is a willingness to be more focused on what *is* rather than on what should be.

I often talk about an open mind, an open heart and an open will as the best way to parent a teen. If we choose to be more open-hearted and make decisions from a place of calm and care, we are halfway to success. Yet, a parent should always be alert to the narcissistic ego that can resurface. We need to be aware of and moderate our thoughts: 'Who does he think he is? I'll show him who's boss in this house! If I let him get away with this, then it's all downhill from here!'

An intentional approach is where we remind ourselves of our core values (authenticity, growth, connectedness, etc.) and tap into our highest wisdom. In this way, we accept responsibility for our behaviour and say, 'I choose to put down this boundary because I think it is the safest option for my son.' This parent wants to facilitate the development of their son's natural self, no matter how different this may be from theirs. It means being fully aligned with who their son truly is, so they rely on techniques of **attunement**, active listening and unconditional acceptance as often as possible. They will look at themselves first before they blame the teen for his behaviour.

A conscious parent will recognise how a teen's decisions are triggering their own unresolved issues. They understand that it is not the teen doing this to the parent, but that it is their own unresolved issues that have been triggered.

Our state of being affects how we parent, and it impacts how we relate to others. I am a strong believer in energetics – if we can discover a calmer state of being, it will have a ripple effect in our homes and in our relationships. If your son is allowed to grow and develop at his own pace, and his challenging behaviour is seen as an important part of his development, then life will become much easier both for the boy and in the home.

The difference between a conscious and an ego-driven parent is that the latter is only concerned with 'doing' – the teen is constantly expected to be doing things to improve academically, socially and on the sports field. Even if society dictates these expectations, as conscious parents we should control how much of this we allow into our homes. The more we buy into doing more, the more we compare our son to others, and in the end we become critical, competitive and controlling – the most dangerous set of Cs, which will end up suffocating our sons.

The 'doing' spiral traps us into focusing on either the past or the future, and we can never be in the present. Everything is about outcome, and it becomes impossible to be in the now and to enjoy the present for what it is. Do not underestimate the pressure of expectation when we want our son to be a 'mini-me' or 'just like your dad', or a fantasy in which our own desires are fulfilled: 'Do this for me!' Such behaviour can be totally unconscious, and it will take time and reflection to discover if it's true about you. Ask yourself:

- What is driving you?
- What is really important to you as a parent?
- Are love and caring important to you as a parent?
- Do all your choices align with this?

Let's get back to the earlier idea of parenting from a deeper wisdom within. I honestly believe that we cannot access this wisdom unless we embark on a journey of conscious parenting and mindful practices.

It is not compulsory to believe that there is a higher self and a higher wisdom. But for me, personally, it's a great resource because I feel that in times of self-reflection, or during expanded meditation or being immersed in nature, I can feel as if I am accessing a higher and much wiser self. But it requires the ability to relax. To calm down. We need to develop the capacity to deliberately seek calmness.

I personally feel that accessing a calm and open state of being is one of our greatest resources, and that we shouldn't underestimate how powerful this can be. And we need to teach our sons how to access their calm inner voice too, because they often suffer from anxiety and worry. They can worry about 'what needs to be done' and whether they are 'good enough'. If we acquire mindfulness, our sons can learn from us how to relax the nervous system so that their higher brain (the prefrontal cortex) can work to access their intuition or deeper knowing.

Ask Megan

Question: *'How do I deal with my teenage son's bad attitude? He refuses to study, he's talking back all the time, and he always has a desire for expensive things. I am a single parent and cannot afford everything. He does his chores at home, but with an attitude and an angry face. How do I deal with him?'*

Answer: *'We have heard a lot about the need to raise boys with greater awareness of their feelings. As women, we judge men who shut down their emotions, who are selfish, egotistical and have poor relationship skills. As moms, we do not want our sons to exhibit these traits. Toxic masculinity results from teaching boys that they are not allowed to express emotion openly. Remember, mentoring and building a good relationship will nourish your teen. Punishment and more anger will not. Part of growing up is learning to be patient without complaining, controlling one's temper, being fair towards others, being sensitive to the feelings of others, and being good sports. In short, part of growing up entails learning self-awareness and acquiring emotional intelligence.'*

Parenting tip from the therapist's couch
I often hear parents say the following:

> *Why is he ignoring me? It's so rude!*
> *He takes so long to do things. It's so irritating!*
> *No one moves until I yell. It makes me mad!*
> *My teens are only ever enthusiastic about their own stuff. It's so selfish!*

The art of parenting is allowing, accepting, appreciating and being open to what's happening in the **#presentmoment**. It's about finding the place of non-resistance inside you. I can hear parents saying, 'So I must just let them do what they want! What good is that going to do?'

But that's not what I'm suggesting. I am recommending that you become more self-aware, and aware of what happens inside you when you resist your teen: do you experience tension, judgement, criticism, resentment, irritation? How does it affect your body, your thoughts, your feelings and your being? Knowing the difference between the following will help you to become more self-aware:

- Having a closed mind full of judgement OR having an open mind filled with curiosity and questions.
- Having a closed heart full of cynicism or rejection OR having an open heart filled with warmth, love and empathy.
- Having a rigid attitude or a stubborn will OR an open willingness to engage, be present and lean in.

If we are without a personal agenda and are open-minded to what is actually happening, the easier it will be to engage with our son and parent wisely.

Worksheet: Homework

Follow this mindfulness practice daily for establishing inner calm:

1. **Set aside some time.** Wake up a little earlier. Get up with the intention to quieten your mind and press pause for 10 minutes.
2. **Be present and sense your breathing.** Be in the now. The best way is to observe your breathing. Feel your breath enter your nostrils and follow the sensation into your lungs. Feel your ribcage expand and your diaphragm drop down.
3. **Let your mind wander and be kind.** Don't judge yourself, and be kind to yourself. If your mind wanders, simply bring your attention back to your breathing. Silence the inner critic.
4. **Return to your breath over and over.** Being present and mindful is a practice, so just keep going. It may help to find a rhythm and breathe in for four counts, hold for four counts and breathe out for six counts.
5. **Be aware of space.** If you are able to access a little calm, then sense the space that surrounds you or visualise a clear blue sky. This can be very calming.
6. **Be grateful and set an intention.** Reflect on three things that you are grateful for in the present moment, and set a realistic and positive intention for the day.

Once you have the hang of this exercise, teach it to your son. Tell him that if he calms down his nervous system by practising this technique, he will be more effective in everything he does..

CHAPTER 11

Bad behaviour: rudeness, defiance, lying, moods, silence

'But emotional sharing was not a big part of my youth. I thought feeling miserable or stressed out was something you tried to ignore, or distract yourself from – usually with drink and drugs.'

– Sam Delaney, 'Our goal is to halve the male suicide rate',
The Guardian, 9 March 2019

Are teens today angrier, more aggressive and worse behaved than before? You hear of kids hitting parents, and parents being afraid of their children. The following are some examples from parents who wrote to me:

'My teen is smoking, stealing and being physically abusive. He claims I'm a bad mom. I don't know what to do to be better.'

'My son is abusing my mother with verbal, cruel words and today he bumped my mother out of the way. Luckily my mother fell on the couch.'

'My son ripped his bedroom blinds down. When his father went in to reprimand him, he threw a lamp at his dad. I had to shout to separate them.'

What is striking about these examples is that parents feel both responsible and guilty. They know it is their responsibility to make things better, but they feel that they don't have the tools to do so.

These parents are not alone. Studies show that aggressive behaviour among teens has increased remarkably. In South Africa, the number of juveniles in high-security prisons is on the increase. Crime and doing harm to others are always linked to angry and aggressive behaviour. Boys are the ones who are blamed for bullying and fighting, yet research shows that almost as many girls are being aggressive at school, although they show it in different ways. Many of our schools are unsafe because of aggression and assaults, and educators are often scared to teach teens. Parents blame the school, and teachers blame the parents.

WHY ARE OUR TEENS SO DISRUPTIVE?

Most psychologists believed that aggressive behaviour was the result of neglectful or angry parents, as well as the teen's daily environment. Boys who feel powerless on the inside do lash out. But why are more boys feeling powerless or vulnerable today? This is the most important question from my point of view. Traditional masculinity is also being questioned. This causes confusion for some boys about 'how to be a man'.

Teenagers who experience or witness anger and violence may become aggressors themselves. Watching violent movies, playing aggressive games, seeing crime in the community and listening to angry music all contribute if experienced on a regular basis. Parents who think that coercing, hitting, insulting or shouting at a child is the way to make them listen, are creating a bully. And those who neglect their children or are overly permissive because they feel helpless raise disruptive, disrespectful teens.

If the school and the parents do not teach the values of respect and consideration, as well as set boundaries and limits, the boys cannot acquire healthy problem-solving skills and emotional regulation.

Ask Megan

Question: '*My sixteen-year-old son has now dropped out of school for good. He is very bright, brilliant at sports and very musical. However, he is violent, beats me up and breaks things. He just wants to play music and is very inconsiderate. His father doesn't want to listen to any suggestions. I am at the point of leaving the marriage, but he has a quiet, caring brother a year younger. I am at my wits' end – nobody seems to have an answer. I am actually afraid of him.*'

Answer: '*A teenager who has become aggressive and violent is scary, and I understand that you are afraid. This boy needs help and not abandonment. Leaving both your sons in the care of someone who does not see this as problem behaviour would be a short-sighted thing to do. Since he has competencies and has dropped out of school, I would suspect drugs or alcohol are involved. Ask him directly if he is taking drugs or drinking. If he is, then I suggest you take him to a drug rehabilitation centre for help. Drugs can cause teens to be irrational and aggressive. It is possible that with love and firm handling this boy may see that he is being irrational. I also suggest that you go to his school and speak to teachers and sports coaches about your son. Maybe you can gather information or help there.*'

HOW TO RESTORE COMMUNICATION DURING AGGRESSIVE BEHAVIOUR

When boys are angry, they often retreat into gaming, especially violent computer games, become sullen, bully others and don't want to communicate. Aggressive adolescents are of great concern to parents and the community at large. Many psychologists working with adolescents believe that positive relationships, not punishment, rescue struggling teens.

Arne Rubinstein, author of *The Making of Men* (2013), agrees that healthy family relationships are key, yet boys also need recognition for their talents and to understand the transition they are going through. They also need to understand the importance of acquiring life skills such as making decisions, setting goals, understanding why emotions are important and communicating them effectively.

I see all aggressive behaviour as a cry for help. A teen boy needs empathy, care, understanding and a strong structure. He also needs to understand why irritability and anger arise in the teenage years. Discuss testosterone influences and anger-management strategies with him.

Some strategies for dealing with your son's aggression:

- Listen to your son. Pay attention to what he says, even if you don't agree. Let him say what he wants to, but don't allow him to just do whatever he wants. Normal limits are always necessary and they are a parent's duty to set.
- Try to forgive both yourself and your teen for what has gone before. Start today with a confident attitude. Be the adult, because you are the one who wants to make changes.
- Stop all aggressive behaviour towards your son. This means no shouting, yelling, insulting or hitting. Boys learn aggression if they witness it in adults. Rather give him clear rules about what you want to see. Let him know during a calm time which behaviours upset you and which behaviours are acceptable.
- Teach him how to manage angry feelings. These types of teens normally battle to calm down and inhibit their aggressive reactions. Teach him how to breathe deeply and calm his body when he first starts to feel angry. Teach him to talk to himself by saying: 'I don't need to be angry. It will alienate me. I must calm down, feel my feelings and find another solution.'
- Do not insult your teen's character, or swear and shout at him. Try to have a conversation where you don't accuse him or shame him. Always calm down first by breathing deeply, taking some time out and widening your perspective before reacting. If you want respect, consideration and kindness, then you need to set the example as the parent.
- Make sure he understands that you will always love him, even if you don't approve of specific behaviours. It's easy for a teen to internalise that he is a bad person.
- Demonstrate problem-solving skills. Talk about how to think about a problem and talk through it, acknowledging different sides. Show him how to resolve conflict and plan a strategy. Brainstorm together to open up to new possibilities.
- Expose your teen to positive role models, especially adult men you admire. Generational intelligence (GQ) is essential to a young man's development. Good adult role models can illustrate how to live a good life. Find books or movies about people who help others and succeed.

- A busy teen is a safe teen. Encourage sport, community volunteering and positive hobbies. Daily exercise, good eating and enough sleep also play a massive role in mental and emotional health.
- Not all serious family problems can be solved without outside help. Counselling or family support groups can be a lifesaver.

The following SWOT analysis is another useful tool for dealing with teen aggression. Teach your son how to use it by simply making a cross on a piece of paper and saying: 'Let's see if we can find a way through this.' Then ask the questions in the diagram. If he gets stuck, encourage him to take it to his desk and ponder a few answers. Then check in with him later. From here, he can set some goals and the steps to reach the goal. This type of goal approach appeals to the male mind and activates testosterone.

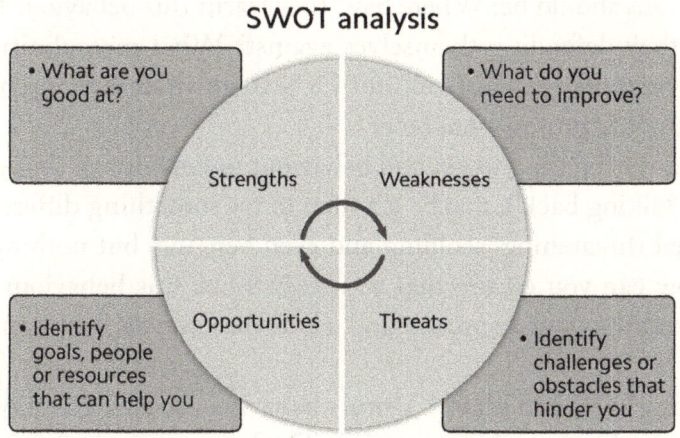

SEVEN COMMON DISCIPLINE MISTAKES

I actually hate the word 'punishment'. Most parents who say 'my son needs discipline' often use punitive approaches in their parenting. They probably spanked their children when they were naughty, told them they were bad, or simply sent them out of the room without an explanation. A punishing approach to discipline focuses on 'Do NOT do this!' and 'I will not like you if you behave this way.' This shames and blames a boy for his behaviour, disconnects him from his relationship with you and, over time, the boy will develop a strong inner critic. Teens need connection, explanations and to be taught healthy options. But just saying 'no' and 'don't' does not help a boy to

amend his disruptive behaviour. Parents need to ask themselves the following questions on how they discipline:
- Why am I so intent on discipline or punishment?
- What am I scared of?
- Am I being over-controlling?
- Could my son's behaviour be a normal part of growing up and asserting himself?
- How can I address his behaviour differently?
- How do I encourage his assertiveness but limit his rudeness?
- What life skills can I help him develop?
- Do we both know how to calm down enough to listen?

Most often, I have found that a teenager's unruly, aggressive or rude behaviour is a **defensive action**. Teenagers are never just nasty people. The important questions should be: Where have they learnt this behaviour from? And what are they defending themselves against? What masculinity messages are being promoted in your culture? Or is there an underlying mental disorder that needs professional help?

If you are struggling to get bad behaviour under control (bullying, lying, cheating, 'talking back'), maybe it's time to try something different. Maybe you've tried threatening, scolding and even begging, but nothing seems to work. How can you ensure that your teen stops this behaviour for good? Time to rethink your approach and avoid these seven common discipline mistakes:

1. **Thinking 'it's just a phase'.** Unruly behaviour doesn't go away. It almost always needs parental intervention. The longer parents wait, the more likely that the behaviour will become a habit. So don't call it a phase: address the behaviour as soon as it starts.
2. **Being a poor behaviour model.** Our behaviour has an enormous influence on our teens. After all, what they see is what they copy. So before parents start planning to change their teen's behaviour, they need to take a serious look at their own.
3. **Not targeting the unwanted behaviour.** It's best to work on improving only one, and never more than two, unwanted behaviour patterns at a time. And the more specific the plan, the better. Don't say, 'He's not behaving.' Instead, narrow the focus to target the specific behaviour you want to adjust: 'He's talking back.'

4. **Having no plan to stop the unwanted behaviour.** Once parents have identified the behaviour, they need a solid plan to stop it. The plan must:
   - address the teen's poor behaviour.
   - state exactly how to correct it.
   - identify the new behaviour to replace it.
   - have a set of consequences if the poor behaviour continues.
5. **Not teaching a substitute behaviour.** No behaviour will change permanently unless the teen is taught a new behaviour to replace it. Think about it: if you tell a teen to stop doing one thing, what will he do instead? Without a substitute, chances are that the teen will revert to using the old misbehaviour.
6. **Going it alone. Big mistake!** After all, if your teen is inflicting the unwanted behaviour on other caregivers – spouse, grandparents, teachers, day-care providers, coaches, scout leaders, babysitters – then you should all unite behind the same plan. The more you work together, the quicker you'll be able to stop the problem behaviour.
7. **Not sticking to the plan long enough.** Learning new habits generally takes a minimum of twenty-one days of repetition. Parents need to commit to changing the bad behaviour and then continue using the plan for at least three weeks. Only then will they see change.

Think about alternative models of maleness. A lot of research on 'being a good man' is available. We need these conversations in the home, and we need to ask our schools to include these dialogues.

Ask Megan
Cutting and aggression
Question: *'My sixteen-year-old was doing okay until high school. Then his marks dropped and his attitude changed. He was in Denmark last year, started cutting himself and started listening to Slipknot. He's okay with my husband, but nasty to me. He has failed so far this year and in certain aspects he has a no-care attitude. He lies about things and always has to be bigger and better. He is very image-conscious.'*

Answer: *'Your son has gone through the worst phase, since he is now sixteen years old. I suggest you do not compare him now with his past behaviour. Your husband needs to play a stronger and more involved role. A troubled boy often copes better when his father becomes more present in his life and does things with him. Dads become all-important for teen boys as they struggle to discover male identity. All the research shows how unruly behaviour and poor school grades improve when fathers show interest in their son's life, friends and schoolwork. I also suggest that his dad and you have a meeting with his teacher, the school counsellor or the principal to discuss a plan of action with his schoolwork. Maybe he needs extra help. It is also important that you check out what is going on at school. Ask him gently but directly what is bothering him at school. Often boys behave in this manner if school has become a distressing place because of bullying, an aggressive teacher or general pressure. Also check if he is using any substances, as this can also cause a sudden attitude change. Lying and being image-conscious are sure signs that your son is feeling powerless and has low confidence. A few sessions with a school counsellor may help. Do not just leave it; be proactive, as this boy needs help, not criticism.'*

Struggling to concentrate
Question: *'My son is sixteen years old and battling at school. He didn't do too well in his June exam and, if he doesn't concentrate on his studies, he will fail. He is very frustrated because he cannot study or, as he says, nothing sinks in. He was diagnosed with ADHD when he was ten years old, but has been fine. He is an active teenager with normal teenage problems, but recently he has been very rebellious and refuses to communicate with us.'*

Answer: *'It sounds as if something has happened at school or in his life. Some ideas: bullying or teasing at school, experimenting with alcohol, girlfriend problems or being involved with something that has gone against his conscience. Try to have a gentle, honest chat with him about what is pressuring him. Include his father in this. At this age, testosterone is surging through the body and it works on restructuring the brain into an adult male brain. Many boys become sluggish and battle with concentration at this stage, and study skills often become a problem as workload increases. I suggest you communicate with the school and find out if any extra lessons or study skills are needed. His ADHD may still be affecting him, and this also needs to be checked by a psychologist or an educational psychologist. Much of what he is experiencing is normal, but does require practical help.'*

Aggression at school
Question: *'How do I talk to my son about his behaviour at school? At home he is a great kid, listens intently, does things out of his own without being asked and is generally just good. At school, however, the teachers are at their wits' end and we have now been summoned to attend a meeting with the school counsellor and the principal because of his aggressive behaviour.'*

Answer: *'This is unusual, as it is often the other way around. Are you or your husband very strict at home? It may be that he feels powerless or intimidated at home, and is taking out his frustration at school. A teen boy of his age needs to feel that he has some control over his own life and that he can make decisions and have choices. Does he have the freedom to do this at home? The aggression at school is a concern, as it is indicative of him becoming a bully. Another suggestion is that something has disrupted him at school and he is lashing out at the system and others. I suggest you allow the school to deal with this. Listen to what the school counsellor has to say and maybe have a few counselling sessions with him to try to discover why your son's behaviour is so different between home and school. If Dad is not intimidating, please ask him to be involved. If your son is a naturally aggressive boy, then I also suggest he increases his sport commitments at school to help him channel his extra energy in a positive direction.'*

HOW DO I DISCIPLINE MY SON WHEN I SEE BEHAVIOUR I DON'T LIKE?

We are so quick to want to stop behaviour we don't like. Most often, what we see as 'bad' behaviour is our son reacting to an event in his environment that he feels is unfair. He may act out or be defensive because he is protesting.

It's impossible to give your son a lecture in the heat of the moment. You are not going to give a good lecture, and he is not going to listen to it. So, your job as parent is to work out how you are going to manage this.

It's fine to pull parental rank – it's all about balance. And it's a good thing to calm down and talk it through, but you have to make it really clear that his behaviour is unacceptable.

Norman Vincent Peale, in his seminal book *The Power of Positive Thinking* (1952), told us that changing our thinking changes our world. Today, I am an ardent believer that raising our consciousness by being more self-aware and intentional in our thoughts and actions has magical outcomes.

So when your son does things you don't like, and it's really rude or aggressive, of course you must correct him. You might say, 'Swearing/shouting is just not acceptable in this house. As long as you are raising your voice at me, I will not listen. The moment you calm down and speak decently to me, my ears will be open.'

But then you have to start sticking to it.

> ### *Worksheet: Using 'happiness science'*
> You want your son to be happy, and enjoy who he is. It seems simple enough, yet there are very few naturally happy teens. There is, however, a huge reservoir of 'happiness science' that works. This can kick-start your positive thinking and enable you to coach your son to access vital life skills:
>
> 1. Think back to the last time you were happy. What were you doing and who were you with? Most often it involved the following:
>   - optimism.
>   - playfulness.
>   - can-do attitude.
>   - connectedness.
>   - sense of control over your life.
>   - good feelings about yourself.
> 2. Do you say things like: 'What will others think? You must get better marks. Life isn't a bowl of cherries.' And then you lecture your son on ethics, morals and discipline. This is quite the opposite of what inspires happiness. Comparison is also a self-esteem killer for a teen.
> 3. Do you often ask: 'So what is the issue? What's wrong?' Are you always focused on problems and issues? This mindset has to change.
> 4. Do you think people should always be happy? Do you search for stimulation and pleasure through events and things? Do you get anxious if your family is in a bad mood? These all promote an anxious mindset and rob you of happiness. Change your thoughts to: contentment comes from within, moods and circumstances come and go, struggles are good, and happiness skills improve resilience.
> 5. What can you do differently? Understand 'happiness science' and apply it. Your mental 'set point' is genetic. This means that we are born with an optimistic and pessimistic bent, but each of us has a different set point – some have a high set point, meaning we are mostly happy; while others have a low set point, meaning they are mostly unhappy. But our happiness level is also offset by circumstances: 40% circumstances and events. The last 12% is choice.

6. What choices can you practise to 'reset' your happiness set point?
   - Three minutes of daily gratitude.
   - Doing random acts of kindness.
   - Smiling more.
   - Laughing more.
   - Taking time out for social connection with people you enjoy.
   - Finding meaningful work or a hobby.
   - Having faith or a belief system.
   - Daily meditation.
   - Learning mindfulness.
   - Using your talents and strengths.
   - Building friendships and secure attachments.
   - Finding spaces to relax, to have fun and to play.
   - Exercising or playing sport.
   - Being in nature, playing with an animal, swimming in water and sitting in the sun.
7. How can you build your son's emotional intelligence? Practise, practise and more practise. Like building muscles in a gym, the more you flex your emotions, the more 'emotional muscle' you'll build. The more consistently you practise, the greater the change you'll experience in what you feel, think and do. Use 'feeling' words, empathise and guess what a friend is feeling. To develop your self-awareness and connection to others and to incorporate this into your life, you need to retrain yourself through hands-on exercises and real-world practise.
8. Finally, try this exercise a few times daily and teach it to your son:
   I feel ...
   I feel like ...
   I feel as if ...
   I feel ... when you ... because ...

Worksheet: Homework

Some mothers report having quiet sons, and they do not experience the rudeness and anger as discussed in the last two chapters. Reflect on the following regarding your quiet son:

Circle 'Yes' or 'No' to answer the following questions about your boy:

Yes   No   Does he have at least one good friend?

Yes   No   Does he have any activity or interest that he really cares about?

Yes   No   Does he talk with adults?

Yes   No   Does he communicate his worries and bad feelings?

Yes   No   Is he doing well in his schoolwork?

Yes   No   Has he shown his sensitive nature from an early age?

Yes   No   Does he ever seem happy – smiling, talking animatedly, making jokes or laughing at them?

Yes   No   Does he get recognition from you or from others for his strengths or accomplishments?

- Did you answer any of the questions with 'No'? If so, reflect on your answer. Has the situation always been as it is now? If not, what has changed and when did that change happen?
- Did any of the questions make you think of something about your boy that you hadn't thought of before? If so, describe it.
- Check all the adjectives below that you feel apply to your son. Add your own at the end of the list.

Funny	Picky	Dependent
Demonstrative	Sweet	Emotional
Talkative	Loving	Smart
Reflective	Trusting	Helpful
Spirited	Curious	Quiet
Intense	Vulnerable	Perceptive
Independent	Tenderhearted	

- Do you think you or the boy's other parent share any of your son's qualities that you just listed? Which ones?
- Do you worry about how your son's qualities will affect his happiness? Why or why not?

CHAPTER 12

Sex and hook-ups on the brain

*'What does it mean to be a sexually healthy man?
And how do you help your boy deal with sexual impulses and risks?'*

Your son's personality, mood, body and entire life are being influenced by a surge of testosterone and a bombardment of erotic media messages. Basically, they've found themselves suddenly in a perfect storm, and it's exciting, yet confusing.

Women do not have the same levels of testosterone; few of us actually understand what it does to our boys. Testosterone is going to rule his life and take over every cell of his body.

Let's take a closer look at how it influences his being.

THE INFLUENCE OF TESTOSTERONE ON YOUR TEEN SON

Testosterone builds muscles, energy, aggression and competitiveness. It has been blamed for bar brawls, extreme sports, gung-ho business deals and too much sex. During the teenage years, the male brain is rewired by testosterone: the teenage brain is becoming a male teenage brain. Experts say that once testosterone really starts impacting, it's like being given six to eight injections of an anabolic steroid every day. At least testosterone production in men is very steady, unlike women's fluctuating production of oestrogen and progesterone.

We know that higher levels of testosterone in a male lead to higher competitive impulses, larger body size, higher libido, more hairiness or sometimes more baldness. We can't do anything about the genetic combination of the patriarchal lineage that comes through our boys' unique combination of genes, but what we must remember is that their environment can influence the performance of genes.

The determination of a boy's character is determined by the interplay between his genes and his environment. Genes will set the predisposition towards, say, being hyper-masculine, but how that manifests depends on the environment, and will be influenced by male role models, the atmosphere at home and at school, the sporting activities chosen … The effect of our genes can literally be switched on and switched off, according to the type of environment those genes find themselves in.

Testosterone production starts at birth and peaks around the age of five, levels out and then fires up again during the teenage years – an 800% increase on what was produced when your son was five. Hardly surprising then that you can feel the testosterone energy when you walk into a room of guys, isn't it? Or even smell it in the air when entering your boy's room?

While the production of testosterone tends to be at a fairly constant level, competitive sports can raise levels and he might become moody and irritable after an intense sporting activity. Aggression in the home – physical violence, even shouting, or things that scare a boy – can also increase testosterone, as well as adrenaline, levels. Really violent homes seem to produce boys with high testosterone and anxiety levels.

A school of excellence, where boys are busy-busy, doing-doing, will promote high levels of alertness. If your son attends such a school, or if his general environment instils in him a sense of being unsafe, it's important that his home situation and the holidays you choose are tranquil and peaceful, where he can feel safe and relaxed. It will allow his system to switch off from always being on high alert. There is so much going on inside him at this time, and he will experience a lot of stress. And stress, for psychologists, is a synonym for anxiety or depression.

At the same time that pimples start sprouting and limbs start getting too long for their body, teenage boys become very fixated on themselves. You will find your son not wanting to undress in front of other boys, locking the bathroom door, closing his bedroom door – he does not want you to see him naked, and he doesn't want to see you naked either.

Size matters throughout the teenage years: 'Why don't I have muscles like the other boys? Why am I so short and he is so tall?' Teenage boys are very conscious of their size compared to the next guy. It can be quite overwhelming, and can cause intense self-consciousness. And then, their sexuality is suddenly switched on!

HOW TO HANDLE ERECTIONS AND MASTURBATION

Play dumb and put a lock on the bathroom door! Jokes aside, boys who have a sudden surge of testosterone can have erections six to eight times a day, without any warning. They could be standing in front of the class when it happens. Understandably, this causes intense embarrassment.

Then there's masturbation. You don't want to hear about it and you don't want to know about it, but there is *a lot* of it going on. You need to come to terms with the fact that this is the by-product of the surge in testosterone – your boy is growing into a man. His sexuality is not out of control, but it can be uncomfortable. Masturbation is sometimes just an expression of curiosity, but it is also a genuine release from the tension in his body. So leave him to it.

For those of you who insist that he doesn't lock the bathroom door when he has a shower, or those of you who shout, 'Get out of the shower!', just be a bit more aware that your son is trying to discover himself in a house where he is being watched the whole time, which can be irritating for him.

For some thirteen-year-olds, puberty won't have been triggered yet; there is still a lot of closeness and a lot of affection between mom and son. But it will come, and suddenly he will feel embarrassed around you and around femininity. Some boys might not want to hug their mothers.

It's an uncomfortable thought, but have you considered that he's afraid of how his body will react? Moms do not take into account that we are women with breasts – and a hug means our breasts are now pressing up against him. He is intensely curious about women, and he suddenly recognises that, 'OMG, my mother is a woman', followed by the worst thought of all for most teen boys: 'Is she still having sex with Dad?' It is overwhelmingly difficult for boys to cope with these thoughts.

And for goodness' sake, do not mock him! At this point he is fragile and self-conscious and unclear about what is going on; if you mock his budding sexuality, it could end in disaster.

TALK ABOUT SEX: IT'S NOW OR NEVER!

By age thirteen or fourteen, most boys have strong sexual feelings and are fascinated by the images of naked bodies. The testosterone now surging through them increases their arousal to any erotic stimuli. They worry about whether they are straight, gay or bisexual. Yet nothing is being done to honour this new part of their life. It's often not even discussed. As a result, boys are full of doubts.

We want our boys to feel good about their sexuality and gender identity. This is where sexual learning comes in. It includes two parts: the physical details of lovemaking, and the much bigger question of attitudes and values. The really potent information about sex is discussing one's attitude towards it. This discussion has to come from parents and the adult community. If you don't talk about sex (and right and wrong behaviour), your son will adopt the values of his friends, and from social media and TV. Be clear and discuss with your son that there is good sex (consensual, respectful, careful about pregnancy or HIV/AIDS) and bad sex (using others selfishly). Some topics to discuss with your son regarding sex and sexuality are the following:

- Puberty.
- The mechanics of reproduction.
- The facts about sexually transmitted infections (STI).
- Your thoughts on teen sex.
- Pornography and sexting.
- Homophobia, gender fluidity and being gay.
- Sex, love, and commitment and marriage.
- Your values and your son's choices.

As boys pass the age of ten, start using sexual words casually and normally in conversation – masturbation, lovemaking, orgasm, as well as the darker ones, such as rape and incest. Talk about consent and how complex that has become. Even if girls say 'No' when they mean 'Yes', it's not up to the male to decide for her. Girls and boys should choose to have sex for the right reason: because they trust and enjoy the relationship. Be more open about sex as a lovely and exciting aspect of life.

Parents must be careful not to drive sexuality underground by teasing him about intimacy. Do talk about it when it comes up in movies or on TV, or in discussions at the table. Demand maturity – with good humour. If you notice your son sniggering or reacting in a silly way to an incident, don't just let it go – ask him about it later, and fill out his understanding. But end the conversation with a joke or a laugh. Give things a more positive spin. The antidote to 'creepiness' is an infusion of warmth, humour and openness.

Sexual needs and gratification experiences are the expressions of the total self, and are intricately woven throughout the fabric of life as a whole. Therefore, the content of the conversations is not as important as the values and attitudes towards sex that you communicate. A good time to talk to your son about sex is:

- After you have seen a movie or news broadcast that deals with sex.
- If someone you know has been raped or sexually abused.
- When you hear a sexual slur ('faggot', 'slut').
- When he shows you sensual social media images.
- When you are talking about your early romantic experiences.
- When talking about your parents' values and rules.

When *not* to talk about sex

Don't ask whether he's 'seeing' anyone. He doesn't want to talk about it. Do you want to know why? He is unsure of his feelings, and you are putting him on the spot about what is going on. You are asking how he's feeling, and how she's feeling. He really doesn't know the answers, so it makes him feel vulnerable. He can't answer you, so don't go there. It's far better for him to come to you when he's worked it out, or has a question he wants to ask. Make sure he knows that you will always be there for him if he wants to talk about it.

AGES AND STAGES OF SEXUAL DEVELOPMENT

Writing on child sexual development, in the *Electronic Journal of Human Sexuality*, Loretta Haroian identified significant developmental milestones that I have studied and verified over the last decade. I have summarised some of my findings together with Haroian's in this section. Note that different boys develop at different ages, and your son may not meet the behaviour suggested below.

At age 11

- There is a lot of teasing of girls, embarrassment about girls, and trying to see nude bodies or look up skirts.
- Discuss with him the physical aspects of bodily functions and how hormones affect boys and girls.
- He may be confused or embarrassed about his growing body. Size matters to him, and a small penis will be of concern to him.

- He will be comparing body parts, and maybe even with girls he knows well.

At age 12
- Boys enjoy a mental challenge and know all the sexual terms, and are more emotional.
- Boys are more interested in hearing and repeating sexual jokes, and in acquiring sexually graphic material.
- They can be embarrassed by sexual situations or jokes, especially if the joke is on them; for example, sexual naivety or ignorance among their peers.
- They are more fully aware that sex occurs for reasons other than reproduction, but tend to think it's dirty.
- They may talk to a parent about sexual matters, but will more often consult the internet or literature for specific information.
- Masturbation increases in frequency, may be experienced alone or in a group, and may or may not result in ejaculation.
- Erections occur with or without external cause and may happen spontaneously at inappropriate moments, causing embarrassment and anxiety about future situations.
- There is a wide range of physical growth taking place, but puberty has normally hit by now. Growth of the penis and scrotum is common and may precede or succeed pubic hair. Pubertal fat is most common at this age, together with 'love handles' and 'man boobs'. Body odour might also increase.
- Gender-fluid boys know they are different, but may still be denying it.

At age 13 and 14
- Heterosexual boys are interested in girls, preferring group activities, yet some fall in love and openly express their affectionate feelings.
- Only about half of the boys have ejaculations before age fourteen, but most know about them.
- Kissing is a favourite activity; however, having a girlfriend or boyfriend is best shown off.
- They may seek sex, but can't ask – they simply see how far they can go.
- If he has sex, he shares it and acquires status among peers as they learn about sex acts.

- Homosexual boys may or may not be involved in sexual activity with peers, but fantasise about other boys.
- Heterosexual boys may think they are gay because they get aroused when up close to their male friends, and may engage in sexual exploration with same-sex peers.

At age 15 and 16
- They now want to work out their own personal sexual attitudes and need information to do so. Boys need to know and discuss the broad spectrum of human sexual behaviour.
- They now have the full complement of adult male hormones without the life experience.
- They don't feel comfortable with their new moods, body, image or sexual feelings.
- Fantasy facilitates arousal and self-pleasure. Their masturbatory frequency increases.
- There is a significantly high and disconcerting frequency of self-reported, risk-taking sexual behaviour, and some have regular sex with girls.
- They may believe that they should be ready for sexual intercourse at every opportunity and that intercourse is the 'best' form of sex.
- Boys unashamedly coerce girls into having sex.
- Gay teens may fall in love, have sex and understand that they are homosexual.
- Managing to have partner sex is problematic for them, even if the partner is willing. Where and when is a major concern, as are birth control and STIs.
- Sexual acts mostly involve touching, kissing, fingering or oral sex.

At age 16 and 17
- Boys' interest in girls increases; porn may be used, but fantasy alone is a reliable and increasing method of initiating the male sexual response cycle.
- Masturbation continues to be the major sexual outlet for most boys; however, kissing and mutual masturbation are favoured activities of even informal pairs.
- Many girls and some boys at this age feel 'they are not ready' for sexual intercourse, but few can explain their criteria for readiness.

- Dating a popular girl means instant status for a boy, but she is expected to 'be there', to wait, to come down on the field after the game, to understand when other things take priority. If she becomes possessive and demanding, the relationship is in jeopardy because the boy loses status if a girl controls him.
- Boys have a stronger tribal sense than girls at this age and want to hang with the guys, but still want a girlfriend, too.
- It becomes clear that sex is much more complicated than function and skill. Sexual needs, gratification patterns and experience are the expressions of the total self, but this is not understood.
- Strong sexual attractions that occur now between homosexual and heterosexual partners can become difficult to contain.

DIFFERENT KINDS OF LOVE

Steve Biddulph, in his book *The Making of Love* (1999), offers parents the following practical advice on the issue of sexual development:

> *'Love, lust, and liking, the three Ls, all play a part in relationships short and long. What our kids, boys and girls, need to be taught is that they are quite different things.'*

Love is wonderful, and often very confusing, too. It is important for boys to know that there are three kinds of attraction:
1. **Liking:** a mind connection – common interests, stimulating.
2. **Loving:** a heart connection – warm, intense, melting, gentle.
3. **Lusting:** a body connection – spicy, hot, hungry, aching, tingling.

Parenting tips from the therapist's couch

Our teen girls are a generation in transition, where gender and sexual choices are more on a continuum, and black-and-white advice no longer works. I've found this generation of girls often demanding about sexual enjoyment, and many boys can misinterpret this as 'loose' behaviour and get confused about boundaries. Girls can enjoy their sexuality – it's not just boys who want to experiment. Some teens are open to **#hookups** and others want commitment. It's super-confusing for a teen boy navigating dating, consent and his own sexuality.

Girls feel disrespected when they sense that their physical attributes are their main value. But what guys find tricky to understand is that there is a lot of pressure on girls to look 'hot', and that they are culturally evaluated by their attractiveness. Also, many teen girls enjoy being flirtatious and to be seen as attractive. When comments or innuendo undermine any skills, intelligence, talent or insights a girl may have, it's seen as harassment.

Girls are hypersensitive about predatory males, and many girls have been parented to protect their boundaries and be outspoken. Yet the confusing bit for your son is that some girls play games, and will seem to accept comments about their body or sexual come-ons at the beginning of a relationship. Some girls find it a fun challenge to 'get the guy'.

Please assume two things: 1) Your teen knows more than you think he does, yet he is insecure or confused about his desires, needs and wants, no matter how confident he may seem. 2) Scoring, kissing and touching are super-fun, but super-complex, too.

So many mixed messages happening! What is a guy to do? The following are some guidelines to help your son check his attitude towards girls and hook-ups:

1. Always speak up about intentions BEFORE any hook-up. If it's just 'having fun', then say so. It may put some girls off, but better than a girl thinking it's serious.
2. Be honest with your compliments. Be kind. If you are authentic, it can't lead girls on.
3. Always give and ask for feedback: 'I enjoy hanging out. You are so kind.' Don't assume a quiet girl means a consensual girl. Ask: 'Do you want to go further?'

4. After any hook-up, no matter how mild, always call to check in or send a message: 'So cool to get to know you.' Also, don't assume that one kiss means that it will happen the next time. Consent is always required.
5. Always repeat that he is *not* available for any long-term relationship if he is not.
6. Girls often remember every word a guy says, and often tell their friends. So he should only ever say what he is happy to have shared.
7. No drunken mistakes, ever! These are always a disaster, and every girl will find it disrespectful and become resentful.
8. If a girl sends a sexy photo or engages in sexting, don't post it on social media. Rather tell her straight not to send them and delete them. (If she is younger than sixteen and your son is two years older, it may be illegal in certain countries to possess this material.)

WHAT MOMS DON'T KNOW ABOUT BOYS AND SEX

When testosterone hits and boys start hanging out in male groups, there is a lot of talk about girls and sex. And it's not always pretty. Boys will objectify girls, talk about which 'yummy-mommy I want to f**k', and swear that they will never put a girl before their male friends. They will say 'bros before hos', and run down any guy who puts a 'chick before a dick'.

The language can be foul in this group, and they collude to operate in a 'code of silence'. A belief system starts to develop about 'girls wanting sex all the time' and that 'the more you force it, the more of a jock you become'. The rape culture began to get traction when boys actually started to believe this teen talk, and carried it into their adult years. Women and girls were seen as sexual objects to use, and the more innocent or needy a girl was for fame, fortune or position, the more these predatory men could assert their dominance.

The #MeToo movement has begun to expose the complex and insidious nature of powerful men believing that it is their right to abuse and use a woman for sex. It has placed global gender inequalities centre stage, making it a subject that you can discuss with your son. Many mothers are now asking me: 'How do I raise a boy to respect women? Should I just ignore the defamatory language about girls or gays? How can I ensure that my boy does not believe he is superior to girls?'

One thing, for sure, is that boys believe deeply ingrained myths about male power and share this with one another in their locker-room speak. Multiple sexual partners are manly. Conquering a girl is your right. 'No' means 'Yes'. A short skirt means that she is asking for it. Mothers need to have conversations in their homes with their husbands, sons and daughters about how patriarchy has ruled our culture for years, and has left many women powerless and unable to advance without 'selling their bodies' or their souls to men. It's up to our sons to intervene when they see their friends bad-mouthing a girl, or turning a girl into a sex object. Encourage them to do this, and don't just shrug it off with 'boys will be boys'.

I know of a mother whose twenty-year-old son went through a gruelling legal hearing because he pursued a girl at work and sent her a number of compliments that were sexually nuanced. The family was pretty broken up over this. It's a subject that mothers need to ponder and discuss. It is new territory for many, and if you live in an old-fashioned, conservative home where the man is the 'king of his castle', you need help fast.

The other time you may need help from an outside expert is if you have been abused by a man as a child or teenager, as it may cause you to overreact to your son's burgeoning sexuality. Talking it through and addressing your feelings will help how you parent your son's sexual attitudes. Your discussions in the home can include the following:

How can a boy flirt and pursue a girl without coming across as a predator?
Is it up to a girl to always have to 'protect herself' when things get hot?
Why can't a boy step down out of decency and respect?
How can a boy listen up when a girl has an opinion he doesn't agree with?

We need to tell our boys that women are not less than men. That girls are not toys to be used for their pleasure. That commenting on a girl's body or pushing her further than she wants to go is both mean and sexual harassment. Maybe it's time to start *asking* if you can hug or kiss your son, and not just assume that you can. Maybe it's time to tell him to stop if he is tickling his sister beyond her threshold. Maybe it's time to have a frank conversation with him about how you are scared of male aggression. Maybe it's time to be honest about how sexual desire can warp judgement, especially when alcohol is involved.

WHAT ABOUT GAY BOYS?

It is not possible to talk about boys' sexual development without taking into account fluid gender identity and bisexual or gay boys. On this issue, the following are some points to consider:

- It is reported that between 10 and 15% of the world's population of men are gay. In other words, we would expect approximately 12 in every 100 boys to have an exclusively gay sexual orientation in adulthood.
- It is not helpful to get involved in a discussion about 'why' boys grow into gay or bisexual adults. In the same way that we would not concern ourselves with the mechanics of why some boys are left-handed, we should not pathologise homosexuality by debating its origins.
- The generally accepted, current medical and psychological view is that genetics may predispose babies to environmental cues that switch on same-sex preferences, and that boys do not just choose their sexual orientation. There is no one gay gene.
- Same-sex sexual attraction can be found throughout nature, so it is not a dysfunction, nor is it contagious.

Even before our children are born, we, as parents, have their lives mapped out for them. And what conservative dreams they are – a career, marriage and grandchildren to sit on our knee! Finding out that your teenage son is gay demolishes several of these hopes, and may replace them with scary images instead. It's natural to feel some grief and concern. Part of the problem in reacting to the idea that your son might be gay is the stereotypes that exist. It is helpful to remember that these stereotypes are not a realistic depiction of the lives of all gay men.

The concerns of parents of a gay son are exactly the same as those of any parent. You want your son to have a happy life. You hope that he will handle his sexuality in a responsible and self-respecting way. And you hope that he will not move away into worlds that are beyond your reach or understanding.

Both heterosexual and gay life can have its toxic side born out of painful circumstances or wounding from negative caretakers. When parents are judgemental or bully their gay or sensitive sons, this shames them and can lead to loneliness and rejection. But if you love and support your son, he will be less likely to drop into self-loathing or despair, and will more likely be self-respecting and responsible about his sexuality.

> **Ask Megan**
>
> **Question:** *'A friend says my son is dating another boy, sometimes dresses as a girl, yet he brings a girl home as his girlfriend. What's going on?'*
>
> **Answer:** *'Gender-identity issues have become more complex by the day and there are many more categories than just male and female, heterosexual and homosexual. We now have people identifying as bigender, transgender, asexual, trigender, pangender, etc. Gender is separate from sexual preference. Many teenagers express themselves as a boy one day and a girl the next, but this does not necessarily dictate their sexual preference. A gender-fluid identity is dynamic and not a fixed point. Ask your teen to explain these concepts to you. They know more about them than we do. This is a true evolutionary change we are experiencing worldwide. My best advice is to stay curious, open and available for conversation, so don't block or judge your teen.'*

> **Worksheet: Homework**
>
> When it comes to sex and teenagers, it is difficult to say exactly what is right or wrong behaviour any more. Sexual attitudes are changing rapidly, and in most cultures sexual experimentation outside of marriage is the norm. Different countries also have different legal age limits for sex. In South Africa, teenagers can legally have sex at age fourteen, as long as the age difference is not more than two years. My best advice is for you to be clear on your viewpoint regarding this issue. The following are a few questions to help you contemplate your attitude towards sex:
>
> - What are your beliefs about sex and how did you learn them?
> - How open and frank are you about sex?
> - Do you feel content about your sex life?
> - Do you think sex should only happen within marriage?
> - Have you chatted to your teens about sexuality?
> - Are you confident about using the words 'vagina' and 'penis'?
> - What messages are you giving your son about sex?
> - At what age do you think your son should have sex?

CHAPTER 13

Alcohol:
The teen drug of choice

'Teenagers can think they're invincible but drinking when too young can damage health and mental well-being.'
– www.drinkaware.co.uk

Most of the Western world is an alcohol-abusing society and culture, and the drug of choice for many. Sometimes we just want to have fun and feel alive. Other times we want the sedative effect of alcohol to dampen sad feelings. We have to ask ourselves what messages we are sending to teen boys that make them think drinking is a necessity, not a choice.

I suggest that you take a strong stance on teen drinking and stick to your boundaries. Some parents believe in allowing teens to have a drink under their supervision, even though this is considered underage drinking. I don't agree with any form of regular underage drinking.

Alcohol also increases the chance of risky behaviour, which includes non-consensual sex. The following are some guidelines to consider:
- Be aware of your teen's access to alcohol in your home.
- Set clear and consistent boundaries, and discuss these with your teen.
- Enforce the limits you set.
- Be conscious of the example you set.

WHAT YOUR BOYS ARE TELLING ME (AND THAT YOU NEED TO KNOW)

I asked a few boys about what they think of drinking and alcohol:

'I think the guys with older brothers in higher grades they sort of look up to, those might be the first guys who think, "Well, he's doing it so it's cool – I should start doing it." They are looking up to the higher grades and trying to act older and be popular. And that's why it's starting, because they have an older brother and they've seen it happen with him and his friends. They have heard their brother talk about how fun that was and what they did and stuff. And I think that's where it starts.'

'In Grade 8, you are seen as a new boy, but in Grade 9 you are nothing and you are trying to act older than you are. You want to try and act out and be more like the older boys.'

'I think it is a subconscious thing, but they end up doing things to try and attract attention. They are acting out.'

'I think it is because they are no longer the new kids in high school. There's a weight off your shoulders. But you're still not a senior. You are stuck in the middle and it's sort of lonely.'

'By the time most of the boys are sixteen, the majority of those who go out a lot will have experimented with alcohol, be it at their parents' home or being influenced at a party or something.'

'It's a sense of growing up, I would say. As teenagers, we tend to need to feel older and that we need to grow up more – sometimes parents treat us like we are still six years old. So it's sort of like, "I am not that kind of person any more. I am growing into myself."'

I also asked where the alcohol would be available:

'First place will be house parties.'

'From their parents' cupboard.'

'It can be really anywhere. You definitely see boys with parents who aren't strict on that and those kids will start bringing it to places and people will want to try it – or they want to fit in with the group.'

Finally, I asked about the guys who say no:

'At the beginning, when it is the in-thing or cool thing to do, if someone says no, then it is accepted – but if you are still trying to make friends or you are still trying to get in that group and be with those guys, it gives you less of a chance to do that because they are doing something that you are refusing to do. The pressure becomes more and people start doing it and then you feel left out and the more people who do it, the more you feel left out.'

'There are a lot of things that come with saying no. You can be labelled; you might not get invited to certain parties because guys think you will snitch. It could also be respected. At the end of the day, if you have a group of friends around you, it is going to be fine.'

'I just completely said no to stuff – you sort of feel left out and you find yourself standing there and thinking, "I'm the only one here who is not doing it, so what's going on? Why am I here?" And you find yourself isolated from everyone else. It's a lot of pressure in a way.'

WHAT DO YOU NEED TO KNOW ABOUT ALCOHOL ABUSE BY TEENS?

Substance abuse is one of the most serious social problems that our community faces. Boys use alcohol because it 'helps them to relax', make friends (especially with girls), gain acceptance and feel grown up.

Alcohol use and abuse have become part of the world in which our boys live and, while you may not allow your son to drink at home, it is a reality that alcohol is available in the clubs our boys frequent and at the parties they attend. It is therefore necessary for us as parents to take certain steps to protect our sons.

As with all parenting choices, how you choose to handle this issue is a personal decision, and these guidelines are not meant to be prescriptive in any way.

Talking to your son about drinking

An open discussion on this topic is essential. Tell your son what your feelings and thoughts are on the use of alcohol by teenagers, and discuss your rules on the use of alcohol. Broach the subject of safe and sensible drinking (the dos and don'ts), as well as the dangers of alcohol use.

Make it clear to your son that choosing not to drink is always an alternative, and that there are good reasons not to drink.

Reasons for adolescents not to drink:
- Alcohol is unsafe for the developing brain.
- Alcohol can damage your brain forever. Take care of it - it's the only one you have!
- The long-term functioning and health of your brain will depend on the choices you make today.
- Your responsible attitude towards alcohol can have a positive influence on your friends and family.

Do not forget that your son needs clear boundaries. As a parent, it is your job and responsibility to provide these. Of course your son will test the boundaries, but you need to stand firm on the rules you make regarding alcohol and drug use, and attending dance clubs and parties.

It is worth remembering that our boys learn by observing and modelling the behaviour of others ... most often you!

Should you allow alcohol at parties?

When making the decision about serving alcohol at your son's parties, ask yourself:

What good reason is there to have alcohol at this party?

Be clear in your mind about what you are trying to achieve by having alcohol available. If it's to be the 'cool' mom, then at least admit it.

The following can cause problems at teenage parties:
- Open parties – no controlled access to the party.
- A lack of parental supervision.
- Partygoers bringing their own alcohol into the venue.

- Alcohol being freely and openly available.
- Partygoers arranging for alcohol to be delivered to the party by an after-hours 'drop-off service'.

The real ingredients for a successful teenage party are the following:
- Strict access control so that only people who have been invited are allowed to attend.
- Security to keep out uninvited guests and to check bags.
- Limited availability of alcohol (or no alcohol at all).
- Parental supervision during the party.

Some parents are of the opinion that allowing boys to drink moderate amounts of alcohol is 'good for them' and 'teaches them to drink responsibly'. *Are you giving your son mixed messages about the use of alcohol?*

Parenting tips from the therapist's couch

I spoke with a mom who has been really worried about her son (fourteen years) drinking, experimenting with marijuana and having 'the odd cigarette'. Before you think, 'That's what happens!', pause and consider this: Could there be other circumstances that need to be taken into account? Maybe this teenager is on serious prescription medication and can get really sick if the medication is compromised?

This mom is feeling desperate, as she carefully monitors her son's health and goes overboard with the right nutrition to keep him emotionally stable and well. He has been doing incredibly well at school, and has awesome friends and healthy hobbies. But how can she communicate and set boundaries that work?

An adolescent's primary driver is **#fittingin** – to be part of a clan and to gain approval and acceptance from it. The approval and acceptance of parents are no longer important. Being a part of the cool gang *and* doing what they do will be way more important. Teenagers find meaning, depth and a huge sense of acceptance by belonging to a tribe of like-minded peers. If the behaviour is anti-authority or slightly risky, then it's even more exciting.

This is an evolutionary driver or impulse that is almost 'hard-wired' inside us, and is more powerful than worrying about health or Mom's concerns. This period of time is a window of opportunity to feel connected and liked, and hugely contributes to a teen's identity and sense of purpose. This drive for peer connection has to happen now and sets him up for young adulthood. Without this peer group, the years ahead will become daunting. During the school years, teens are forced together into a diverse group that they did not voluntarily choose, which teaches them essential social skills like getting along. It also establishes identity formation. Young adulthood cannot happen without it, as it's a much lonelier world out there when school is over.

This particular mom found it really useful to reflect on her own teen years, and what had made her happy. For her, it had been belonging to a particular group she would have done anything to be part of. We spoke about what it felt like when the group smoked a 'joint', and what it felt like to be the only one to say 'No', and what impact that had.

So, where does that leave you? Do you allow your teen to do what they want to fit in? No! But just knowing how powerful that connection 'driver' is may help you to understand why your teen may lie, remain silent or go against your wishes. His need to be liked by the group takes first place.

So, do put in place boundaries and say 'No', but have an understanding heart? Do reflect on the stuff you got up to in your teen years. How did it feel, and why was it so vital? Have this conversation with your teen – at last he will feel that you understand.

THE TEEN BRAIN ON ALCOHOL

When alcohol enters the body, 20% is absorbed immediately and the other 80% is absorbed in the small intestine. The heart pumps the absorbed alcohol to every part of the body, including the central nervous system, which consists of the brain and spinal cord. It travels to the brain quickly and that's why, even after just one drink, you can feel light-headed or relaxed.

Alcohol acts primarily on the nerve cells and interferes with communication between nerves and all other cells, slowing everything down. And that's why, when we drink even a little, we experience the effects of alcohol on our emotions, judgement, balance, memory, speech and anger levels, just to name a few.

Alcohol can do irreversible damage to various parts of our brains, as research by, among others, the Turning Point Alcohol and Drug Centre has shown. Binge-drinking (five or more drinks in a row) is the most dangerous type of drinking, and has become a worldwide trend. It can become a real problem from age eighteen and older, as it increases the risk of serious consequences, as well as brain damage.

Any form of drinking affects the cerebral cortex, which controls our senses and inhibitory centres, which is why, when you drink, you become more talkative, more self-confident and less inhibited. It also affects our thought processes and our ability to make good judgements or think clearly.

The brain's frontal lobes control our ability to plan, form ideas, make decisions and exercise self-control. When alcohol affects the frontal lobes of the brain, you may find it hard to control your emotions and urges, and you may act without thinking. You may even sometimes become violent or act completely out of character.

The cerebellum controls our coordination, speech and balance, so you may have trouble with these skills when you drink alcohol. People affected by alcohol sometimes can't walk properly or can lose their balance.

The hippocampus is the part of the brain where memory resides. When alcohol reaches the hippocampus, you may have trouble remembering something you just heard or, even worse, have a blackout and not be able to remember what you did at all. If alcohol damages the hippocampus, you may find it hard to learn or remember things in the future.

The hypothalamus is the small part of the brain and performs an amazing number of the body's housekeeping chores. After a person drinks alcohol, blood pressure, hunger, thirst and the urge to urinate increase, while body temperature and heart rate decrease.

And, finally, the medulla oblongata controls the body's automatic actions, such as your heartbeat. It also keeps the body at the right temperature. Because alcohol chills the body, drinking a lot of alcohol outdoors in cold weather can cause a person's body temperature to fall below normal. This dangerous condition is called hypothermia, and can ultimately lead to a person's death.

(**Note:** Brain science is changing rapidly. This information from the Turning Point Alcohol and Drug Centre in Australia was accurate at the time of going to print.)

Encouraging natural highs

I love the idea of introducing 'natural highs' as a family. If we want to change the habitual idea that alcohol is fun, we need to explore ways of enjoying ourselves without it:
- Finding value in a job well done.
- Hiking up a mountain.
- Kissing someone.
- Receiving a warm hug or a smile.
- Eating or cooking a great meal.
- Doing an aerobics class.
- Winning a match or game.
- Hang-gliding or bungee-jumping.
- Watching a good movie.
- Listening to music.
- Creating a piece of art.
- Downhill skiing or mountain biking.
- Volunteering at a charity.
- Practising gratitude daily.

Based on what you enjoy doing, are there experiences that you think could yield the same kind of 'natural high' for your boy? Can you think of ways to make them happen more regularly?

There is a diverse pattern of alcohol usage among teenagers globally. But all countries in the Western world have one thing in common: before the end of high school, almost all teens would have tried alcohol. This is why parents need to be informed and watch their own alcohol use around their sons.

If I could repeat my parenting days, I would have allowed some experimentation, but would have been much stricter on frequency and quantities regarding my sons' drinking habits. I also would have discussed the link between 'being a man' and drinking. 'Drinking with the boys' still has a weird status among teen boys. By discussing the topic, you help your son question his thinking and find other, more meaningful, group activities.

> ***Worksheet: Homework***
>
> Discuss with your partner whether you agree or disagree with these statements, and create your family policy on alcohol:
> - When boys are growing up, it is normal for them to try out alcohol. Agree/Disagree
> - It is sensible for parents to allow their boys to drink alcohol. Agree/Disagree
> - Allowing young boys to consume alcohol in moderation and under supervision teaches them to drink responsibly. Agree/Disagree
>
> You will also need to decide on the following:
> - At what age am I comfortable for my son to start drinking?
> - Where and under what circumstances is it acceptable for my son to drink?
> - When do I want my son to start buying his own alcohol?
> - What do I want my son to know about alcohol and drug use?
>
> Some psychologists believe drinking is a normal part of socialisation that enables teenagers to experiment with and acquire adult behaviour, that complete abstinence is as deviant as excessive drinking, and that in our society drinking alcohol in moderation is normal.
>
> Do you and your family agree with these beliefs? Have you discussed them?

CHAPTER 14

Addiction issues and suicide

'Not why the addiction, but why the pain.'

Why on earth do teens use chemicals? And this includes alcohol, which should be seen as a drug.

The reasons can include that addiction runs in the family, psychological pressure ('I hate myself. Something's wrong with me') or social pressure ('Nobody likes me. I don't really fit in. Everyone's doing it').

The trigger could also be as simple as availability. A boy I had once counselled had walked out of a shopping centre and over the road, was offered a Mandrax pill, took it, and subsequently started smoking dope and got hooked. That is how easy it is to get addicted.

Commonly, teenagers smoke cannabis, sniff glue and abuse prescription medications as recreational drugs. Cocaine usage is fairly low compared to alcohol abuse, but this increases in wealthier sectors of society. Heroin is a drug that keeps cropping up in all social circles, and crystal methamphetamine (also known as 'tik') use is massive in South Africa, with crack being more common in America. Steroids are certainly also abused.

So, what are the basic motives of taking any form of chemical? Expanded awareness, thrill-seeking, new experiences, to fit in, to be accepted by their peers … You can see why teenagers would love chemicals.

Another reason for some is that drugs blot out reality. Michael Gurian, in his book *Saving Our Sons* (2017), says: 'Millions of our sons are living with little or no purpose, failing to launch.' Substances can therefore be a quick fix and an escape from their problems, including feeling shame and unworthiness. One teenager told me that it felt 'like a million angels from heaven were hugging me' the first time she used heroin. You can see how it would be an incredible temptation for someone who just wants to get away from their life.

ADDICTION ISSUES AND SUICIDE

We joke about retail therapy, but even shopping can become an addiction, when you need it to feel good about yourself, or are using it as an escape. Watching TV, consuming porn on the internet, gambling and eating can all become addictions … Power, wealth, fame, even emotions themselves can become addictive. It is not only the drug that the addict needs. It's the high from the drug; it's the positive emotion that is desired.

Why do some people get addicted and others don't? No matter what your son is like, you are probably experiencing this fear. I hope to unpack the issue for you in this chapter and lessen your fears. Ask yourself: Could my son get addicted? Could he (or I) consume too much? Could he (or I) be an alcoholic?

HOW DOES ADDICTION WORK?

Gabor Mate says that 'all addictions – whether to drugs or to non-drug behaviors – share the same brain circuits and brain chemicals. On the biochemical level the purpose of all addictions is to create an altered physiological state in the brain.' (from: *In the Realm of Hungry Ghosts*).

The brain is not just a whole lot of wiring linked together. Neurons have gaps with receptors at each end. Receptors need chemical messages to do their job. And all emotions have chemical messengers. Serotonin, dopamine and the other neuropeptides rush around these little gaps and then fit to these receptors. The hormones that trigger our anger, stress and happiness are exactly the same ones that are triggered by drugs. The drug uses what we already have, and then amplifies the effect.

We need to understand the compatibility of our bodies and our emotions to these chemicals. The centre of the brain is the limbic system. That is where your pleasure centres lie and where all your dopamine and serotonin stimulation is going to happen. Your brain circuitry for pleasure is triggered when a drug or addictive behaviour is introduced. Food can stimulate dopamine production, as will cocaine. Sex also produces quite a high dopamine rush. But heroin has the greatest effect, and that is why, once a person is addicted to heroin, it is so difficult to come off it.

Why are some people predisposed to addiction and others not? Is it the environment? Perhaps biology? Or the brain mechanism? If a close relative was addicted to alcohol or any form of drug, you have a 25% greater chance of becoming addicted than someone else. If someone in your family is an alcoholic, it is a good idea to discuss it with your son and warn him against this genetic predisposition.

Many parents, however, turn a blind eye. They don't want to start a conversation about alcohol and drugs. Yet research shows that parents can make a difference simply by engaging their sons in conversation. Sometimes we can be very moral, and when there's a problem, we blame bad friends, or the club culture, or too much money, or the availability of drugs. Instead, let us face facts – that our teens can be tempted into using drugs – and openly discuss it with them.

WHAT DO *YOU* NEED TO KNOW ABOUT DRUGS?

Your two enemies are ignorance and denial. As a parent, you are up against the increased availability of drugs, society's attitude to alcohol/drugs, the club culture, the prevalence of anxiety and depression disorders, the highly competitive and stressful environment we live in, and your children's access to money. Arming yourself with knowledge is half the battle won. Use the following lists to check for signs of drug use at home and at school.

Signs of drug use at home
- Avoiding family activities and responsibilities.
- Changes in appetite, mood and complexion.
- Valuable items/money disappearing.
- Coming home very late or not at all.
- Being secretive; unusual behaviour.
- Spending a lot of time alone.
- Lying about activities.
- Finding the following in the house: cigarette rolling papers, pipes, small glass vials, small plastic bank bags, remnants of drugs (seeds, powder, etc.).

Signs of drug use at school
- A drop in grades; teachers complain.
- Loss of interest in learning.
- Sleeping in or bunking class.
- Poor work performance.
- Poor attitude towards sports or other extracurricular activities.

- Spending a lot of time alone.
- Reduced memory and attention span.
- Not informing you of school activities.

Physical and emotional signs
- Suddenly changing friends.
- Uncharacteristic behaviour.
- Being negative, argumentative, paranoid, anxious or confused.
- Destructive behaviour.
- Overreacting to criticism.
- Being overly tired or hyperactive.
- Drastic weight loss or gain.
- Being unhappy/depressed or having severe mood swings.
- Deterioration in standards of personal hygiene and appearance.

SPORT AND SUBSTANCES

From the side of the rugby field, the big schoolboy can look so fierce and in control. Is he just showing a tough face to the world? Boys and men are measured as successful when they perform well on the sports field or in the boardroom. To maintain this image of strong masculinity, a boy may turn to steroids to keep the perfect six-pack or to stay on the team.

Steroids are adaptogens that affect hormones. They are bad for the body, but have become popular because they improve endurance, strength and muscle mass. Injuries, mood swings, acne, stunted growth and increased risk of heart disease are common side effects of the regular use of steroids. Not to mention that a teen is messing with a body that is still growing!

Tim Jarvis, a counsellor at a large all-boys boarding school, asks: 'Why are boys so intent on being big and better that they will harm themselves?' He suggests that our culture needs to redefine what strength actually is. He is helping boys to look at their definitions of masculinity and to talk about it.

> **REMEMBER:** The force of authority is not enough to stop your son from using!

Ask Megan

Question: 'My friend phoned me this morning to tell me that she caught my sixteen-year-old son smoking. My son and her daughter are friends. How do I approach him about this?'

Answer: 'In my experience, when parents who have good relationships with their children find out that their teens are doing stuff that they do not know about, it's a shock. It's a shock because of the awareness that your child is growing up and that you are no longer fully in the feedback loop of their activities. Friends become all-important and secrets are kept from the family. Most of the time the secrets are not anything to be concerned about, because it's simply fun to do things on their own, as it helps teens feel grown up and a little "in charge" of their own lives. Parents overparent their teens these days – they have become the most monitored generation ever. As parents, we need to find the balance between giving freedom and setting limits. This is the most difficult aspect of raising a teenager, because there are no hard-and-fast rules; it depends on the trust levels and communication in the relationship.'

WHAT CAN YOU DO?

Expect that your teenager is going to experiment with things you will not like! You can counteract this by being well informed yourself. Don't be naive or ignorant, and talk to your son about drugs. Find out what gives him that feeling of euphoria, and rather encourage 'natural highs' (see the examples on page 192 in Chapter 13). The following are more strategies to consider:

- Practise tolerance and an open-door policy. Most teenagers only try smoking once or twice and then decide that it's not for them.
- Decide, with your parenting partner, on the limits you are going to set around substances. Expect your teen to push the boundaries sometimes, and decide on which privileges you will take away. Or offer some incentives for positive behaviour.
- Educate yourself on the facts around alcohol and drug use, and share these with your son.
- Accept that your teen can SAY anything they want to at home without you reacting, but they cannot DO anything they want to. Make it clear what behaviour you expect.

- When it comes to smoking, take a stand and share the facts about the damage it causes. Just simply saying 'No' and overreacting will not stop it. Rather listen to your son, share your feelings, opinions and reasons, and give him the facts about smoking.
- Most teenagers will continue to do what their parents harshly disagree with. Therefore, your tone of voice and how you approach the subject will be all-important. Appealing to his rational side and finding a way to get his cooperation will require ingenuity and creativity. (I know a health-conscious mother who purposely bought a packet of cigarettes and started smoking in front of her teenager in confined areas to drive home a point. The teen thought his mother looked so gross that it shocked him into reality.)
- Find out what the school's smoking and drug policy is and inform your teenager about it.
- Do be aware of the crowd your teenager hangs out with. If they all smoke, he will be under peer pressure to try it, too. Have a conversation about finding ways to say 'No', and the strength it takes to honour your own integrity.

TEEN SUICIDE AND HOW WE CAN HELP

We worry a lot about addiction, and yet there is another form of self-harm that is on the rise among male youth. Depression and suicide rates are rising sharply globally. For the first time in South Africa, we are seeing a rise in suicide among urban black youth. In this country, it's easy to blame family breakdown, high crime rates, high unemployment among youth or poverty, but with suicide rates rising worldwide, this explanation is not complete.

Australia has named mental health as the biggest adolescent issue, even above drugs and substance abuse. The Australian Bureau of Statistics (2017) says: 'Deaths from intentional self-harm occur among males at a rate more than three times greater than that for females' (www.abs.gov.au/ausstats). Suicide has thus become the leading cause of death for youth in Australia and other Western countries.

In the US, it seems one in eight teenagers has experienced a major depressive episode. Feelings of sadness, anxiety and hopelessness have begun to rise since 2008. A national survey on drug use and health collected data from 600 000 youths to verify this sad news (www.time.com/5550803/depression-suicide-rates-youth/). There is an increase in mental health issues among American youth as well. But why?

Depression, bipolar disorder and high anxiety are often causes of suicide. These are mental health issues, and are often a combination of genetics and a stressful environment. The predisposition to develop depression can also be passed on. Most psychological research shows that the genetic risk of developing clinical depression is about 40% if a biological parent has been diagnosed with the illness, with the remaining 60% being due to external factors in the teen's environment. Depression is unlikely to show up without stressful life events, but the risk of developing depression as a result of such an event is strongly determined by genetics.

But that's not all. Certain personalities are also more prone to depression or anxiety. Being a person who overly worries, who is a perfectionist, or who is very shy or socially sensitive can also contribute to developing depression. Sometimes medication is needed, and almost always professional help is essential for dealing with mental illness.

The impact of the dominant culture

Research by psychologists such as Michael Gurian (*Saving Our Sons*, 2017), Warren Farrell (*The Boy Crisis*, 2019), Arne Rubinstein (*The Making of Men*, 2013), and Dan Kindlon and Michael Thompson (*Raising Cain*, 1999) highlights a pressing issue – that the masculine culture is an emotional straitjacket for boys that narrows their choices and causes mental health problems. Boys are expected to perform, to provide and to succeed, no matter the costs. Although patriarchy has enabled males to be more powerful and make more money than females, it is also a gilded cage. Men are shamed for being mediocre or for not climbing the hierarchy of success.

Although abusive and power-hungry male behaviour needs to change, boys and men are battling to find an alternative way. No one can dispute that boys and men often fake their strength, as they are under constant pressure to prove that they are tough and in control. This robs boys of an empathic, authentic and soulful life.

As mothers, we need to know that male empathy and expression is different from that of females, but it is no less real or important. We need to understand that masculinity is in transition and causing complexities that are difficult to navigate. It is important to encourage our sons to be more emotionally communicative, contributory and accountable. Mostly, they need a caring and nurturing male role model.

The impact of technology and information overload

Suicide and its causes can be a complex question to answer. Extreme external stressors, as cited above, can trigger suicidal tendencies, but they are not the only causes. One issue that needs to be addressed is the impact that technology and social media has on the youth, as their use has risen alongside depression and suicide.

Research shows that heavy technology use is becoming a serious problem. Teenagers spend less time with friends and being outdoors and more time indoors on social media. To me, it's more a case of encouraging some outdoor living and healthy socialising, but I worry about the overload of information teens endure. The youth never used to be so well-informed about the ravages of war, the starvation of children in Africa or the death of hundreds in unexplained aviation disasters. It's tough enough for them to be concerned about their own local issues, but now they are exposed to suffering from all around the world. Constant images of distress can really upset and unsettle us, even as adults – for teens, it is even worse.

Technology is also affecting how teenagers date and socialise, how they navigate their identity formation, how they imagine the future, and how they view the world. *Adolescence is a time of trying to fit in and to connect, and social media sets up a relentless comparative culture.* It's tough to be okay with an ordinary life when so many young people around you are showing off their fabulousness. But, as with all things, it's how teenagers are coached to manage this stress that will give them the tools to deal with it.

Instead of pointing fingers at technology and social media as the cause of teen suicide, we need to help our teens manage their stress and build their own competencies. Resilience is about building a positive vision of your future, noticing your own strengths, and deciding what you can change and what you can't. Then, getting on with your plan to work on what you *do* have control over.

Other triggers for suicide

There are different triggers for different personalities, but it's essential that, as parents, we are aware what aspects of life are important to a teen – relationships, music, sport, academics, his body and appearance, his place among his peers ... If these things are 'going wrong', it will have a huge impact on his mood and self-esteem.

Teenagers hate feelings of failure, or embarrassing themselves or being left out. They are deeply affected by family turmoil or being bullied or rejected. Any form of abuse, be it emotional, financial or sexual, is dangerous for their mental health. There are so many external stressors that can affect a vulnerable teen, but there are professionals, medication, and skills- and stress-management techniques that can help. The following are some strategies for when a teen is contemplating 'ending it all':

- Take it seriously and ask what they plan to do. Be direct.
- Listen and allow them just to talk without giving advice.
- Check that they are safe. Are there weapons in your home?
  Don't leave a suicidal teen alone.
- Get help and support. Even if it turns out to be a false alarm,
  it's worth speaking to a professional.
- Always follow up. And get support for yourself, too.
- Do not allow yourself to blame the family or yourself. A distressed teen and poor mental health can be due to a genetic cause or a chemical imbalance, and not be anyone's fault.

LIVING A MEANINGFUL LIFE

Prevention is better than cure. Knowing that suicide is a risk among teenagers can galvanise you into action. A sense of meaning and belonging is essential to a fully lived and grounded life. A teenager needs to believe his life has meaning, and it's important that we lead by example. Our past structures and systems of 'finding meaning' have diminished, as many people no longer turn to the church, their pastor or God for help.

As adult guides, we need to explore our wisdom about life and share it with our teens. Start by building your intrinsic values. Those values you believe in, no matter what others say. Establishing a few intrinsic values that are meaningful to you will create fulfilment. It could be as simple as: 'I like doing small tasks of spontaneous giving,' or 'Engaging with my passion makes me feel alive.'

Offer your teen some life skills, too. I advise parents to use the three life tools of *I can*, *I have*, *I will* to build resilience. Every teen can be encouraged to have an 'I can' attitude. Look out for a victim mentality, and help your teen recognise his strengths and his own unique characteristics. Remind him of his internal and external resources: 'I have friends, a strong dad, a loving friend, a rugby team who believes in me, a helpline I can call.'

Also keep reminding him of the 'I am'. This is your deep sense of worth, the essence of who you are and the values that you uphold. The 'I am' can also be seen as your life force, which needs to shine for you to really feel alive. As you age, the 'I am' becomes a part of your soul or your calling in life. These three tools can help a boy overcome fear, which is vital in overcoming stress.

Finding meaning in life and the 'I am' takes time, a sense of purpose and a process of self-discovery. It requires us to go out into the world but to always check in with those we love and care about. We need to do that in our teen years, too.

A wise adult is one who has identified their passions and motivation for doing things, yet who is still flexible and open to new experiences. We need to continually revisit our purpose and vision in life, and update it every few years. This means that we need time to reflect and to turn our dreams into action if we want to lead an intentional life.

But it's not all about dreaming and choosing ways to express these dreams; it's also about developing the skill set that we need to support our choices. What do *you* still need to learn? What skill do you need to develop to live out your ideals? Sometimes it's going back to school, or finding a mentor or doing an online course. Life is for living and growing – it helps us live a meaningful life. We should also celebrate the little steps of improvement we make. Find ways to measure your progress, and take time to share and enjoy it. Do the same for your son. Surprise him with a small family celebration at home to mark the progress he has made in something.

Carl Jung suggested that living a meaningful life requires us to connect to something greater than ourselves. For some, this may be a code of honour, an organisation, a business you believe in, or it may be religion, something spiritual or a higher power. I have always found deep satisfaction in nature, and also being in silence. I feel restored when I spend time alone in natural ecosystems and wide, open spaces. I love connecting to trees, to the earth, to water and to the sky. It softens and opens my heart, and I feel a deep connection to natural cycles that have sustained us since the beginning of time.

I'm a great believer in mindfulness and meditation, too. Doing this in silence has served me well. Having an open heart and open mind has helped me to forgive those who have caused me harm, and has enabled me to move into a place of abiding acceptance. My practices of meditation, breath work and yoga have helped me lessen the stress and tension that often build up from a busy life.

When I'm back in a balance of *mind-body-soul*, it's easier to soften and be available to my life from a calm centre. This also helps me to reflect and find clarity of thought. I would highly recommend finding practices that calm and restore you. If all else fails, just get outdoors, breathe, take your shoes off and feel the earth, behold the stars or stroke your pets. Nature soothes and reminds us again and again of what is most important in life.

CULTIVATING A GOOD RELATIONSHIP WITH YOUR SON

As adults and parents, are we willing to consider new information, ideas and perspectives, and keep our hearts open? This will aid your relationship with your son, and a good relationship can keep a boy safe. If he values his connection to you and/or to his dad, it will enable him to try to rise above his teenage stressors and urges. I'm not suggesting that a good relationship alone will prevent suicidal ideation or action, but it may help him open up to you.

Empowered and grounded mothers are pivotal in helping a boy to be comfortable in his own skin. We need to find a way to have a mutually satisfying relationship, one that offers love and appreciation, but also provides good life skills. If we become more attuned to our intuition and trust in it, it will enable us to drop our agendas and defences and be honest and authentic with our sons. We need to find the courage that will enable his progress towards manhood, no matter how much he rejects or criticises us.

As wise mothers, we choose to participate in his life. We can lean in and we are curious about who he is becoming. We find ways to have fun, to laugh and to do stuff together. We don't just interrogate, question and watch him. We participate in his life and in his interests if and when required.

Of course he won't want you to be totally involved in his life, but make an effort to find those activities that you can share. I got my skipper's licence, bought a boat and spent hours being a skipper and driver while my sons water-skied. Yes, I did have to camp, make fires and schlep all sorts of picnic food to remote dams, but it was worth every second. Sometimes I lost it, sometimes I cried and sometimes I was exhausted, but being a part of their fun was always exhilarating.

We can't just theorise about having a good relationship with our sons. We have to get out there and do it and experience it. To be fully attuned to another person takes time, and we need to drop our agendas to do so. The one thing you will always be able to give is your attention. What type of attention do you choose to give? Is it hard and critical? Or soft and open?

Another aspect you can always control is your attitude. Your feelings may come and go, and a situation may change, but it's your attitude towards something that can make all the difference. So reflect on where your attention is, and what attitude you bring. Boys love fun and, if you have a sense of humour, it's really easy to engage them.

TEENS AND THE SEARCH FOR MEANING

Teenagers are at the beginning of their search for meaning. When the adults around them live a meaningful life, it helps them immensely. Teenagers can take a long time to mature into their passions and intentions, as they are still exploring who and what they want to be.

Let's look at some tips for what teens need to find meaning in their lives. They need to:

- express their aliveness through vital action (dance, sport, art, song).
- satisfy their need to connect to their own peer group.
- have a meaningful connection to something greater than themselves (a good school, a wholesome charity or club, God).
- exercise free will and discover their own agency (do things on their own).
- be able to explore and make mistakes (without being judged or made to feel guilt).
- master something that they are good at (maybe outside of school).
- have at least one adult who cares about and believes in them.

Parents meet these needs by:

- Attunement – being able to truly listen to your son from his point of view and putting your relationship with him first, before asking for performance.
- Recognising him on a deep level – really seeing him without your own agenda and expectations.
- Open listening – dropping the chatter in your own head, opening your

heart and mind, accepting where he is at and allowing him to talk without shame.
- Quality of presence – being present and open, and finding that centre within yourself that is calm and appreciative of what is.
- Setting appropriate boundaries – being soft and open does not mean being a walkover. You are the mother, the adult and the guide. You are the wise woman who respects herself and stands up for what she believes in. Be clear and be responsible for yourself, and expect the same from your son.

Be clear about the values and ethics you live by, and be able to explain why. Be curious about a well-lived life and be willing to imagine yours. What do you aspire to? What are you growing within yourself? How does this inspire you? What skills do you need as a mother to help your son tune into that which is meaningful to him?

If you are concerned about your teen, do not ask him if he wants to talk to someone. Take him to talk to a counsellor or psychologist. If you think your teen is suffering, it is your responsibility to get help. Do not assume that your child is 'grown-up enough' to make his own decisions regarding this matter. You are the parent, and it is still *your* responsibility. Of course, your teen may be extremely resistant or hostile, or even blame you and tell you it's a waste of money, etc., but do not be intimidated. Let the professional worry about the teen's resistance. After all, that's the person's job!

Worksheet: Homework

Read through the symptom checklist and tick 'Yes' or 'No' if you notice this behaviour more than 50% of the time that you are with your son: Is there a valid reason for this behaviour, or are you noticing it almost every day (for more than a month)? If you have ticked 'Yes' to more than one symptom, please have a look at the guidelines at the end of this section.

SYMPTOM	YES	NO
Evidence of the depression triangle – pessimistic about himself, the future and the world in general		
Worrying and being anxious or tense with physical symptoms		
Compulsive behaviours		
Obsessive thinking about people, events, possibilities		
PTSD symptoms with stress reactions		
Feelings of persistent sadness and hopelessness		
Withdrawing from friends and previously enjoyed activities, and feeling alienated		
Showing increased irritability or agitation		
Changes in eating or sleeping patterns		
Having low energy or motivation and lacking concentration		
Evidence of recurring themes of death and suicide		
Associating with a negative peer group or using the 'dark Web'		

If you notice one or more of the symptoms on the checklist:
- Don't minimise your concerns.
- Don't think all that is needed is reassurance.
- Be patient with your teenager, but not with the situation.
- Keep the channels open, especially for support and help.
- Listen, listen and listen some more.
- Compliment your teenager on his strengths.
- Don't hesitate to talk to school personnel, or a professional, if you suspect that your child might harm himself or others (there will be lots of time later to apologise if you acted in error); a lifetime is often not enough to make up for not acting on what turns out to be a valid concern.

CHAPTER 15

Screens, porn and sexting

'Scoring a nude photo from a girl can feel like a conquest.'

– Sixteen-year-old boy

Mothers around the world have the same complaint these days: 'Why is my son so obsessed with his phone?' In order to answer this question, let's put this generation into context.

Generation Z are the present teenagers, born after 1995. There are about two billion of them in the world, and they make up around 7% of the South African population. They are digitally savvy and difficult to engage, since they live in an 'on-demand' world of infinite choice. They have been called the 'mobile first' generation, since they were almost born with a phone in their hand, and they are very engaged with social media and online shopping via their phones.

There is no doubt that all our different screens affect the way we perceive ourselves and interact with the world. Research into this phenomenon is rapidly growing, but it has only just begun. The problem is that while psychologists are studying a particular pattern, the next technological influence is already breaking onto the market. Things are changing too fast to keep up.

Phone and screen usage can be compared to any addictive behaviour. Each beep, bing and 'like' raises arousal levels, and causes a high dopamine release in the brain that is addictive. This dopamine release means that when you tell your son to 'shut it off', he suffers withdrawal symptoms – a big comedown or meltdown. Technology is so alluring, exciting and stimulating that the 'high' is very high. This is in sharp contrast to the kind of withdrawal a teen would get when you say they can't ride their bike or read a book.

You may notice that withdrawal results in irritability, moaning, weeping and sometimes anger. Do you recognise any of these signs in your son? If your teen takes no time off from his screens, then it means he is exhibiting habitual usage. This will cause an impact on his mental, emotional and physical health.

HOW DOES TECHNOLOGY IMPACT YOUR SON'S BRAIN?

As a psychologist, what interests me is the impact technology has on the psyche and personality:

What is the impact of this technology on the human brain?
Are social media and cyber contact affecting a teen's social conditioning?
Are screens altering us, and how?
How is the formation of the ego and identity being impacted by the cyber personality?
Is cyber social-profiling and cyber social-imaging promoting narcissism?

Answers to these questions are not complete, but we do have some insight. Chronic gaming shows up on an MRI scan as increased blood flow to the deeper parts of the brain, and results in hyperstimulation of the stress response. Defensive reactions result, and the frontal cortex is no longer in charge. The prefrontal and frontal cortex helps to regulate mood, and is home to our executive, higher functioning. This area of the brain is not being stimulated while gaming, so in a way it is switching off. If this continues, it increases anxiety, ADHD, depression and self-harming tendencies. The teen then struggles to regulate himself.

DOES TECHNOLOGY HAVE AN IMPACT ON CONCENTRATION?

I read an alarming article a few years ago about research on brain waves, and how they synch with and are altered by our cellphone signals. This suggests that we are becoming attuned to our phones and laptops in a structural way that can be measured in brain waves. Research regarding newborns and music has shown how quickly brain waves can attune to outside sounds and movement. In fact, neuroscientists have shown that the rapid pacing of movies is affecting teens' learning ability and attention span. Kids who watch movies often are showing a 60% drop in learning ability.

These findings have fuelled an entire psychological view – the addictive patterning and abusive usage of our personal technology (PT). There is also a lot of research showing that our concentration abilities are being affected. The present teens are said to only have a concentration span of eight seconds! Information presented to them must be short, sharp and to the point. They always want facts, but in point form, and are able to move through loads of different information fast. A concern is that these teens think they know information when they have memorised some bullet points. They will, however, seldom contemplate or reflect on the information.

The workplace is also showing signs that technology is interfering with our concentration. Focused work and long hours of concentration are tough for young millennials, and will be worse for Generation Z, who are still to reach the job market.

WHAT CAN YOU DO?

Poor concentration will affect studying and exam time. There must be a new approach that uses different senses. A teen's visual sense is well formed by PT and, therefore, listening to a lecture, or using creative drawing skills, or speaking out loud when studying, will help your teen maintain concentration. Use of the other senses, like sound, smell, voice and touch, will also help expand memory.

I highly recommend that teens create charts and drawings, make notes by hand, read their notes aloud, talk them through with a friend or tutor, or even record their voice or their teacher to listen to at a later stage. Even using modelling putty on a board, as a creative way of highlighting points or facts, is useful. Different colours can be used for different aspects of a subject that need to be remembered. Drawing on an artist's talents through song, movement and even painting will help improve concentration and memory.

Memory can be stimulated by different senses in different ways, and our brain has various pathways for knowledge acquired through our various senses. This allows for a more whole-brain approach to studying. What is missing among these teens is the skill of reflection and contemplation, which require the frontal and prefrontal cortex. Screens, gaming and most visual images use the mid- and hindbrain. Taking time to think and savour things is done by the right brain and the cortex. How we feel and interpret a subject requires a higher-order thinking.

The frontal cortex is still growing during the teen years, and the prefrontal cortex is only fully developed by the early twenties. This part of the brain controls concentration, but is also in charge of executive functions like decision-making, deductive thinking and setting intentions. It also calms impulses, so teens who are alive to their impulse drivers are relying on their mid- and hindbrain – the very area stimulated by screens. Practising contemplation through time in nature, journalling or even talking through material with a friend will help teens to practise being in 'real' time, and to engage with higher-order thinking.

How can we parent in an IT-savvy way?

- Include your teen in setting rules. Ask them what they think a reasonable time limit should be for screen time.
- Get your teen's buy-in. Explain (not lecture) the neural impacts of technology and addiction patterns.
- Be the mentor and not the monitor. Don't be authoritarian. Teens will appreciate the limits if handled with a firm but fair approach.
- Put the do into the don't. Express what you really value and want: 'I miss connecting and engaging together. I'd love to spend time with you doing something or chatting.'
- Notice what your fears are about when your son sits in front of a screen non-stop: is it that your teen will miss out? Or that your teen dislikes you?
- If your teen is showing extreme reactions and withdrawal symptoms, then it's time for extreme measures. Enforce a cyber fast: no media, no phone, no tablet, no laptop, no screen of any kind. Some experts suggest a fast of three to four weeks. Even one switch-off day has shown remarkable results – better concentration, improved social skills, better sleep and calmer moods.

What moms say about screen time

'I try and get my son's cellphone out of his room an hour before he goes to sleep. Then I switch the Wi-Fi off for all our sakes. It's hard because if I'm totally honest, we are all addicted to cyber. I use this as an excuse for some downtime for myself. I think we have all given in to media usage to give ourselves a break. It has taken over quite a bit in our house.'

'We have a rule of no devices at the dinner table, and it makes meals last long, be chatty and fun.'

'I have found that our teens love playing a board game or a card game or building a puzzle, but often are prompted only when I've clamped down on cyber time.'

'I take a retreat every year for my mental, emotional and spiritual health, and I must confess that last year I spent almost every night checking my phone! It has become an extension of my way of being.'

'I admit a little shamefully that cyber time is slightly out of control in our house. I try to limit it, but not consistently enough (so it becomes arbitrary to them), and if I were honest, it is likely they are probably modelling their behaviour on mine!'

'I'm a bit of a headmistress about this ... Lots of charts in my house with clear times when specific things are supposed to happen. Sounds dull and strict, I know, but because I include the fun stuff, everyone knows when they can get on their screens, so I get minimal push-back ... For now!'

'I arrived at a house the other weekend and it was deathly quiet! Why? Mom and Dad were on laptops, teens on their phones and the little one watching cartoons on a tablet, all at once. I was a bit shocked and yet, at the same time, could appreciate Sunday silence! To change this pattern would involve a huge parental effort of game-playing, or a weekend away, or storytelling, or inviting another family over. It seems we are unable to be bored or individually creative at the same time.'

'Parental opposition against cyber time seems as reactionary as when my parents are against something. My father saw my smoking as satanic. We live in a multichoice world, so if you want your kids to have more options, provide them with some that match the adrenaline fix that computer games provide. A weekend in the country without lights and TV will soon be unique.'

'Every now and again I impose a time-out. I put all connection appliances into a box at, say, six p.m., and close the lid. I think they all (including the adults) hate me briefly, but ultimately feel quite relieved that I've taken it on.'

'I need to be beaten with a stick on this one. Totally addicted to the point that I haven't read a book in ages.'

Do rules and restrictions work?

The more rules, limits and restrictions you put in place and monitor, the more your teen will feel that he is 'on probation' and in a home prison. Try switching to mentoring – make time for discussions and explain your values and the reasons why you prefer certain behaviours rather than others. Lead by example, and give them the space to self-monitor.

It is worth monitoring what they're doing online, and also mentoring them in navigating the digital world. While there are no hard-and-fast rules, it is up to us to advise them on healthy usage, and to offer the tools they'll need to live balanced, fulfilling lives. We all need to learn how to use technology without being used up and addicted by it!

But if our teens are becoming addicted to their screens and social media, what about pornography and sexting?

ARE OUR TEEN BOYS ADDICTED TO PORN?

This is a huge fear for mothers, even though many parents turn a blind eye to their son's pornography usage. Male adolescents are naturally sexually curious, and visual cues are the most enticing for the imagination. Our sons and daughters are the first generation of teens engaging with pornography as they are growing up. Porn sites get more visitors each month than Netflix, Amazon and Twitter combined, with Pornhub alone receiving 21.2 billion visits in 2015 (www.huffpost.com/entry/internet-porn-stats_n_3187682).

Is it a social experiment that is causing irreversible harm to their brains, behaviour and attitude towards sex, or will it just become normalised and no big deal?

The biggest danger lies in these sex sites becoming the 'go-to place' for sexual education, especially if parents are not discussing sex in the home. And if pornography becomes the only education platform, what are our boys learning?

According to Prof. Gail Dines, our boys are discovering sexual interactions; how gender is played out in sexual relationships; what constitutes sexual consent (or lack thereof); and the normalisation of gendered violence (https://digitalcommons.uri.edu/dignity/vol2/iss3/3). And then we were wondering where the 'rape culture' could be coming from?

In a 2017 study, it was found that if you consume pornography frequently, you are more likely to hold attitudes conducive to sexual aggression and engage in actual acts of sexual aggression than if you did not (www.researchgate.net/publication/288905229).

For mothers, I think the most distressing fact is that our boys are learning stereotypical gender roles via the viewing of pornography. Women's bodies, as depicted in porn, are totally unrealistic and objectified, with most scenes depicting a willing and subservient female partner. If a boy begins to think this is normal, his sexual satisfaction and relationships with normal girls will be negatively affected. Some research is even revealing that boys and men who frequent porn sites cannot get sexually aroused without the use of visual pornography cues.

WHAT ABOUT SEXTING?

Sexting is a common phenomenon and involves a teenager sending or receiving sexual photographs or messages from another teen. Teenagers want to take risks and they want to be popular, and they are convinced that sexting assists them in this. In America, 28% of teenagers say they do it and, sadly, most pictures are sent on to another person. Research shows that the act of sexting does not cause teenagers emotional harm, yet the non-consensual dissemination of an image does. It is an act of betrayal and causes emotional and psychological harm to the victim.

I have personally heard of at least five cases where young teen girls sent nude pictures of themselves to boys in the hope of starting a relationship, or to keep the boy interested in her. The plan backfired and the pictures went viral, causing almost irreversible trauma to the girls. One girl, now in her twenties, told me that after eight years, she is slowly recovering. Teenagers can be cruel and mocking, and these sexual pictures are used for cyber bullying.

Sometimes it happens because of experimentation and curiosity, and at other times because of pressure from a potential boyfriend or girlfriend. Researchers have found that boys request and forward sexual photos and messages to a greater degree than girls. This is important for mothers to know, because many mothers of sons will accuse girls of being sexual predators.

WHAT CAN YOU DO?

Mothers need to have courageous conversations with their sons. They need to ask in a forthright manner about porn usage and highlight the dangers and impact that it has on their development. If this is not possible, at least do not turn a blind eye. Give him articles to read, motivate his school to engage boys on the facts and consequences of pornography, or go and see a professional together.

Talk openly about how pressurising girls to consent to sexual acts can result in harassment. Also speak about the dangers of sexting and how it can ruin one's reputation for years, and may even impact a future career. Discuss how girls' reputations are more negatively affected than boys', and that it is important to care about their friends and have respect for girls.

In many instances, sending sexual messages can have legal complications, and you should familiarise yourself and your son with this information. Is your son aware of the consequences of all his actions, sexual and otherwise?

Worksheet: Homework

Collaborate to work out your family's view on porn and sexting. Set boundaries and discuss the consequences of not meeting the family values. Use the following questions to achieve this:

- How much sexual freedom should your son have?
- Is it his right to express his sexuality in the way he chooses?
- How do you feel about your son receiving a sext from an admirer?
- And how do you feel about him sending a sext of himself?
- Do you have filters on your home computers?
- Should you monitor your son's phone and laptop?
- What is your attitude towards pornography usage?
- What rules do you have in place in the home?
- Have you ever used pornography for sexual arousal?
- Should your son be allowed to watch some porn?
- Does your son know the impact of porn on his emotional and sexual well-being?

CHAPTER 16

Real issues that moms have

'Sometimes I feel like it is an impossible and thankless task. The world I grew up in is so different from my son's. Everything is more complex, and most of the time I'm not sure what to do!'

– Mother of a seventeen-year-old boy

REACHING A SULLEN TEEN BOY

Question: *'My son's father and I differ on parenting styles – we are divorced. Our son is sulky, surly and withdrawn. He yo-yos between social behaviour and total withdrawal behind headphones or shut doors. This is followed by surly rudeness and he is blind to anyone else's needs. His father seems desperate to please and very seldom sets boundaries or requests good manners. He leaves me to take on the discipline and to be the "bad" cop.'*

Answer: This situation sounds familiar to most parents of teens, and the opposing forces within one set of parents are always fascinating.

Reaching a teen boy who has withdrawn into himself or becomes silent is tough. The first thing to understand is that it's most often not his fault, and he is not purposefully trying to hurt the parent. He is normally under assault from feelings, thoughts and motives that he is not clear about.

This is unpleasant for you, but a necessary phase for a boy who is trying to assert himself and grow up. **A boy needs to 'grow up' emotionally, mentally and physically, and he needs to 'show up' for himself, his friends and his family, and eventually he needs to 'stand up' for his beliefs and values.**

A divorced dad may be desperate to please his son and will very seldom set boundaries or request good manners, leaving the other adult to take on the discipline and be the 'bad' cop. I often find that an insecure parent, unsure of his or her role, becomes vague and ambiguous as a parent, resorting to seeking some kind of approval from the teen that will tip the power balance in their favour. The teen is then free to do as he pleases, and this leads to a breakdown of boundaries.

If a parent is feeling insecure, they may resort to being the 'cool' mom or dad, and try desperately to get the teen to like them. They claim that they 'only want my teen to be happy'. But at what cost? A need for affirmation and approval then dominates their parenting.

So, a parent whose self-esteem is shaky becomes an over-pleaser. Teens subconsciously, and sometimes even consciously, sense the lack of boundaries set by the weak parent, and claim their 'power' over the parent. There's nothing a teen boy likes more than pseudo-power and fake bravado. He instantly feels bigger and bolder, and does not have to go through the struggle of finding his own competency. But this defiance of hierarchies is an essential process for the maturing young male to go through. Earning respect and status is what helps a teen boy to discover his place among men. A teen that has experienced a whiff of freedom to 'do as I want to' or knows that the adult male in his life is incapable of 'telling him what to do' won't turn back. It's a downhill ride from there.

It may seem unfair, **but by the time your son is a teen, you need to have matured into an adult, or you will be mauled by a stampeding teen.** Nature intended it to be like this! A midlife mom and dad should have the self-awareness, clarity and moral compass of a mature adult to parent appropriately.

TEACHING BOYS TO RESPECT GIRLS

Question: '*How can we raise our sons to respect women? And what can I do at home?*'

Answer: Respect is about valuing a woman's qualities, and acknowledging her needs, skills and worth, even if she is 'different'. Sexual harassment has had lots of relevant press. For our sons, this subject can be distilled as follows: respecting girls is accepting that 'no is no', and that a girl is not just a body to grab!

Disrespect of women is a learnt behaviour. It's not inherent that men are superior and women are inferior. Obviously, upbringing and home dynamics can play a huge role. Fixed mindsets, gender stereotypes, prejudices and cultural beliefs run very deep. In fact, so deep that sometimes we don't notice when women are being put down or made to feel 'less-than'.

A teen boy can generally be rude or test his assertiveness by ordering his mom or sister around. This does not mean he has turned into a harassing male. It means he is a teenager and testing his male boundaries (or doing what he has observed). It's experimental at age eleven to fifteen, and moms and daughters should speak up and say that they don't like it. By the end of the sixteenth year (and if a growth spurt has occurred), disrespect can begin taking root, and some moms have reported being scared of their sons' aggression.

So what can you do? The following are tips for teaching boys to respect and honour women:

- Our homes need to demonstrate respect for and kindness to all. If a father demeans a mother, obviously it's not a good example. The best that the mom can do is to at least say to her teen, 'I don't like the way Dad talks to me, and I hope you don't treat girls like that.'
- Do not 'serve' your son, and do not expect your daughter to serve him.
- A mom can idealise a son or put him on a pedestal – be aware of doing this. Turning your son into a little prince is a breeding ground for narcissistic traits.
- Hold your son accountable for his mistakes or poor behaviour. Don't let him off the hook by saying 'boys will be boys'.
- Have the conversation! What is respect for women? What is gender inequality? Why is the rape culture so harmful? Look for examples in your everyday life.
- If your son is using demeaning names for girls or objectifying their bodies, speak up and name it.
- Talk about male and female stereotypes – name it. Boys may enjoy being protective and that's okay, if you are okay with it.
- Consent and harassment are very serious legal issues, and boys need to understand that self-control and sexual self-regulation are essential.

HAVING A CIVILISED CONVERSATION

Question: *'I approach my son with the best of intentions and want to have a civilised conversation. But it always seems to break down into the same situation – I scream at him and he blanks me.'*

Answer: Is your agenda ruining your conversation? It is almost always because we have an agenda. And that agenda normally involves finding out information, venting frustrations, moralising, having a gossip, giving instructions and – the one teens dislike the most – lecturing them. So what can you do? The following are a few good ways to have a civilised conversation:

- Be interested in what your teen has to say.
- Be conscious of the quality of your attention (be open and willing).
- Listen without getting ready to follow your agenda.
- Ask how, what, where and when questions.
- Don't jump to conclusions. Rather ask a straight question and slow down. If you feel your pulse rate rising, simply say, 'I need a minute. Let me think about it.'
- Lean in and dialogue. Debating is like ping-pong; rather be curious and interested to discover something together.
- Share your feelings, be real, be funny, be kind and stay present – your steady and open presence is half the art of conversation.

Finally, my best advice is that one day you may discover that your teen was your best teacher and that you are the grateful student. What conversation have you had that was a learning curve for you?

LEARNING HOW TO FIGHT 'RIGHT'

Question: *'My son always wants a fight! It feels as if life is a permanent argument and we are continually fighting about stuff both big and small.'*

Answer: The following are some tips for learning how to fight right:
- Your teen is not the enemy. You bat for the same team. Keep reminding yourself that no one is out to get you, even when it feels that way.
- Slow things down! You are in control, so try to talk about one thing at a time. Purposefully say 'No' to all the extra arguments he is throwing in the mix, so that you lessen your load.

- Become really aware of your body. Move it, stretch it, let it rest! Then check in with your breath and posture regularly, so that in the heat of the moment you are able to relax when necessary. Being ready to fight shows up in your body or posture first.
- Practise self-talk: 'I'm okay. My relationships are best kept loving! This, too, shall pass.'
- Don't bring up all the hot issues in one go. Once we get heated, we can easily drag up the past. Some issues cannot be resolved and require professional help. Know how to spot these.
- Encourage yourself to pause before reacting or being super-critical and angry. Visualise the last time you all had a good day. Linger on happy thoughts. Increase your appreciation for anything that's going well.

BEING POSITIVE AND BREAKING OUT OF THE 'NEGAVERSE'

Question: *'I feel like I am always the bad cop in our house. I am always telling my son what he is doing wrong. I want to kick myself. But I do it again the next time. How can I have fun with him rather than always being the dragon?'*

Answer: We have a habit of noticing everything that's wrong. We have a tendency to look out for all that is negative before we appreciate the positive. It's a hard-wiring we have that serves as a survival instinct.

As parents, we are quick to ask what's wrong (albeit with deep sincerity). We will spend an enormous amount of time researching a symptom or attitude that appears to be a problem. We seek out the best treatments, therapists and tutors to sort out all those 'issues' – all the things we consider not good enough.

And so we tend to live in the 'negaverse' that points out all that is 'not enough'. Our children's grades aren't good enough, dinner wasn't quite right, our relationships aren't good enough, and of course there's never enough money or time! Psychologists have discovered that being positive is not a normal default position. It's a practice!

And a worthwhile practice to break us out of the 'negaverse'? To appreciate just what *is*. To resist the urge to say, 'So you got a B. Now where's the A?' To drop the comparisons and just like our loved ones as they are right now. To be grateful over and over again for a smile, a warm breeze, a blue sky, a family meal, a hug, or just that your teen is home.

Practise saying something positive or encouraging:

So nice to have you home.
That was a kind thing to do.
I love spending time with you.

DEALING WITH CLASHING PERSONALITIES

Question: *'I clash with my son. We have always had what I would call a "personality conflict". We simply can't see eye to eye on anything. I often catch myself thinking that I don't really like him, and that really scares me.'*

Answer: It is not uncommon to find that you are not a good personality fit with your teen. It's a concept that child developmental psychologists discovered years ago. We are all born with a temperament or 'energy level'. Does your temperament match or 'fit' with your teen?

Think of a simple example: Do you engage with life as an introvert or extrovert? If you have a highly energised, assertive and outgoing teen and you are more cautious, careful and struggle with change, then there's a good chance you will clash about how you approach things.

I remember a teacher telling me that I overstimulate my son, and that he performs much better when I'm away. I was devastated. It was so hard to hear this, and I felt powerless at the time. But I slowly learnt that he did not react well to change, excitement and tardiness. He needed me to plan better and tell him in advance what was happening, so he could prepare himself emotionally.

We should be prepared to look at our own style, and step back and observe at what pace and how often our teen prefers activities to happen. I suggest you both complete a personality quiz, such as the Myers-Briggs personality test. Take time to compare results and discuss ways in which you can accept and appreciate your differences more. Another good tip is to find an active hobby that you both enjoy – being with a teen boy in an active way takes away the necessity to talk in order to get along.

HANDLING THE NEED FOR INDEPENDENCE

Question: *'My son is so selfish and I really think he owes us, but he does not think so. He says it's time to do his own thing. I think he should still do what we do as a family. Any advice?'*

Answer: Check in with your beliefs and attitude first. To name and claim does not infer a relationship. To see your son as 'yours' as he grows towards his manhood is to keep him trapped in his co-dependency on you, the mother. He needs to discover his own agency.

Another factor also arises when we feel we 'own' our children – parental entitlement. We feel that he owes us and that he should meet our expectations of him. This assumption can set up a relationship of 'power' over your son, and it can become difficult for him to establish his own individuality and independence. This will remain unconscious in both of you, until you are honest with yourself. Ownership mentality is also about the ego; the idea that we have created our sons and that they must listen to us all the time is egotistical.

Ideally, you should find a balance. How can you set your son free to discover his own agency, yet also ask him to be a responsible part of the family or the community? This is one of the fine lines you experience when parenting a teen, and it requires us to be both wise and mature. We need to understand his need to explore his own values, beliefs and identity, as well as let him leave the family nest for a while, trusting that he will return as a valuable part of the family. All of this takes time, but we need to trust this process as a natural part of growing up. We also need to name it and say to our son: 'I understand that you need your freedom to explore, but remember that you are also a son, a brother and an important member of our clan.'

I love to use nature's examples to help us parent in a natural and organic way. In nature a species or plant can spring into life and be fully itself, but it still needs to adapt to its niche. As humans, we are also hard-wired for connection. Our brains operate best as social beings. All natural systems, including the family, have a reciprocal, adaptive relationship with its niche. This metaphor of nature may help you explain to your son that as he branches out from the family, he is still nourished by the trunk.

DEALING WITH SELFISHNESS

Question: '*He is so lazy! I can't stand it. What can I do?*'

Answer: You have to remember the steps to conscious parenting. Is this behaviour actually appropriate and normal? Yes, because teens are self-focused and need downtime.

You can't discipline a dog for wagging its tail. It's the same with an adolescent. You can't overdiscipline just because you think that selfishness is completely unacceptable. It is completely normal. It is part of ego formation, and relates to your son trying to find his identity.

You can remind him of when he did something good, and keep on praising him when he is kind, gentle, goal-focused, considerate and does his homework. So, praise and affirm the things that you like to see him do (even though that might only be one or two things in the beginning). And highlight the things you would like to see done (for example, clearing the table after supper).

HANDLING HOMEWORK

Question: '*My teen struggles with homework, yet he used to be quite organised. What is going on?*'

Answer: Teens get brain fog at about the age of thirteen or fourteen, just when you thought you needn't manage their homework any more They can even seem to have suddenly become ADHD. Yet it's just a normal growth phase.

The brain is about to experience its last growth phase before adulthood, which affects the prefrontal cortex, the executive area dedicated to organisational skills, planning, deduction and impulse-control. Although the brain continues to grow right into the early twenties, I have found that after age sixteen or seventeen, brain fog suddenly lifts and your teen becomes much more confident of his abilities.

HANDLING CLIMATE-COLLAPSE PARANOIA

Question: '*My son is paranoid about climate change. He calls it climate collapse! He says that we are not doing enough as a family while the planet is being* *destroyed and that his future will not be a life of quality. What can we do without causing him or his sister more anxiety?'*

Answer: This is an issue really close to my heart, and the best approach is to have a plan of action as a family. First off, know the facts. Read up on the scientific data and don't get caught up in the crossfire of so-called *climate deniers*. Well-established conservationists like the World Wildlife Fund (WWF) or Conservation International have good newsletters. Personally, I like the website skepticalscience.com.

Your next step is to contemplate how you feel. The information on climate change is overwhelming and can cause feelings of panic or despair for all of you. Listen to your son, yet be the adult and keep calm. Talk to other families about how you feel, and check in with the school sustainability projects to see how you can get involved as a family.

Develop a positive attitude about how your family will work as a team to make a contribution. Place the emphasis on sharing, caring and becoming aware of the impact of the things that you use in the home or in the environment. It's not just about reduce, reuse and recycle. It is about being mindful of and grateful for all our natural resources.

Facilitate 'nature connection' as often as you can. It improves health and well-being and inspires the 'conservationist' in your teenagers to do something. The trees, animals, water, air and sun calm us, broaden our perspective, enhance empathy, improve our mood and offer a sense of meaning. Time in nature remedies ADHD and anxiety disorders, and relieves depression and even social anxiety! So declutter, unplug and switch off. Take your eyes from the screen and to the horizon; your feet out of your shoes to bare earth; your bodies to air as you jump off warm rock into natural pools; find the big blue skies, the ocean depths, or the endless stars of a dark and quiet night. Take your teens to where the nightjars call. All your answers will flow once you prioritise weekends and holidays for nature connection.

Final thoughts

I have a lot to say and a lot of advice to give, yet I cannot claim to be the perfect mother. It was difficult for me to be present, open and responsive. I tried and failed and tried again. My mistakes and failures taught me more than my successes did. These concluding reflections are about how my struggles fostered my parenting approach.

I am the mother of two sons, two grown-up men whom I adore with all my heart. When we set out on this journey together I was young and reactive, doing what I thought was right, but mainly following a textbook (Marina Petropulos's *Baby and Child Care Handbook*) and the advice of a very strict paediatrician. I was living on a farm much too far from support, was sleep-deprived and had a relentless inner critic. I deferred frequently, thinking everyone else was right and I was wrong. I managed to gather a local group of mothers and I set up a STEP programme in my home.

Right here is my first hard-earned lesson for new mothers: **Don't do this on your own**. Get help. Reach out. Practise self-care and always remember to value your position as a mother. Do whatever it takes to educate and empower yourself. Find ways to thrive.

Thankfully, my innate love and my desire to raise happy children kept me on track. I wanted us to laugh, to play and to enjoy each other. I wanted to be outdoors, in nature, and to give my active boys the space they needed to explore. I had a natural longing to transform the mundane into an interesting experience. This kept us sane during the dark years of separation and divorce.

Lesson number two: **always protect and focus on the essentials first**. As mothers, we are happiest when our children are safe and happy. Promote happiness, laughter and enjoyment. Build bonds through play and creativity. Nature is healing and also offers boys exploration space. Even big boys like to play.

Another complex struggle for me was that I was not only a mother. I was a single woman, too, with a yearning to have a career I could be proud of, to establish my own identity, and to love and be loved. My life was a dynamic mix of moving parts that could easily have torn my sons and me apart. I wanted a life, and so did they. With humility I can say that a fierce grace must have intervened with a good idea. I completed a master's degree in psychology and later launched my parent courses while my sons were still in high school. The research with other parents strengthened my resolve as a mother and I began to see a clear parenting path. This included dialogues, collaboration, understanding masculinity, acknowledging teenage needs and creating a home that was boy-friendly.

Big lesson three: **spend time finding creative ways to meet your goals, and make them teen-friendly, too.** Expand your knowledge of adolescence and masculinity and create a home that may not look perfect, but is functional for teenagers. Buy earplugs, play your own music louder, have your own friends over and enjoy your home. Nurture an independent life that synchronises with your family's.

Maybe the courses became popular and lasted for over ten years because I needed them as much as they needed me. I learnt how to be a mother of sons with the help of other parents. This, in turn, I discussed with my sons, asking their advice. They got involved. The knowledge and encouragement I received from other parents helped me to look honestly at myself. Through my studies as a psychologist and my interactions and therapy sessions with young boys and girls, I began to 'get' adolescence. This strengthened the bonds between my sons and me, as I tried to articulate where I thought I had gone wrong as a parent and, more importantly, we began to be much more open and authentic with each other. The joy I have received from our interconnected lives weaves a precious pattern in my heart.

Big lesson four: **talking to your sons about your struggles – within reason – allows them to contribute where they can.** Operate and dialogue as a team, but remain the adult. Interact with their friends and welcome other parents into your home. Mind the gap by studying, reading up, and listening to podcasts about teens and their generational issues. There are great online courses and interactive workshops for parents. Do them. But avoid trying to be the cool mom, the pleasing mom or the yummy mommy, no matter how it strokes your ego. It's unhelpful and embarrassing.

By reflecting on the hundreds of parents who have consulted with me as a professional psychologist and parent expert, I have realised that there is a pattern to their concerns. Some query their parenting skills: Have I done right by my boy? What am I not seeing? How can I do better? These parents feel guilt.

Some query their son: Is he okay? Is this behaviour normal? Why is he so lazy and disinterested? Why does he not speak to me? How can I get him to do the right thing? These parents finger-point.

Some are insightful, open to change and forward thinking: 'Tell me what I need to do.' They set goals and have a mission. Sadly, others might be stuck in the past: 'I never raised him to be like this!' Or, 'Do you know how difficult it has been?' They remain victims. I have listened to these questions and tried to answer them for you in this book. I hope you have seen your habitual patterns and felt your vulnerabilities, as this is where the fertile ground lies. Our struggles are the seeds from which we can harvest our strengths.

Whatever your style and whatever your way, the most effective rule of thumb is to pause, calm down and be present. Lean into your feelings, listen to what he is saying and sense what he is not saying. And then love. **Always return to love**. Love and forgive yourself first, and then open your heart to your family. Love and an open heart will heal all relationship wrongs.

Nowadays, I meditate every morning. I practise mindfulness, do gratitude exercises, spend time in nature and have a Buddhist practice called *Metta*, a loving-kindness meditation focused on developing unconditional goodwill towards all beings. *Metta* has taught me the joys of self-compassion and to offer compassion to others. Finding peace is a practice.

Looking back over the years of raising my boys, I have a positive bias and a selective memory. I see the good things and the good times, but believe me when I say that I floundered and cried and had outbursts once a month and sometimes felt like a victim. I got confused; I felt overwhelmed and failed to maintain a healthy work–life balance. I chose some poor love relationships that had my boys rolling their eyes. I often felt guilty and had spurts of over-fixing and over-supplying. Yet we all managed to be authentic, playful, honest, loyal and connected. We also made time to enjoy many weekend adventures together.

Another big lesson that blossomed from dark places, and which I now teach, is to set an intention. **A clear parental intention that is based on shared values**. Discuss these values and allow everyone's voice to be heard. Action

FINAL THOUGHTS

them and put the 'do' into the 'don't'. Always stay connected to your and your son's core values, no matter what the effort. And be warned: never become a slave to your son.

I have also collected tips from other parents. At my courses I always ask, 'What works for you and what doesn't?' I evaluate most courses and ask for feedback. In this way I have gathered advice from the mothers and fathers of boys and girls. I have edited these lists for you and written them in the worksheet on the next page. Read them. Ponder them. Add to them and, most importantly, make them your own. Practise doing something differently, or 'fake it until you make it'.

There is nothing more satisfying and empowering than to have a solid and deep relationship with your son that will stand the test of time. A relationship that inspires his own and empowers his emotional health. A son who calls to say hi; who prioritises your birthday; who loves to come to your home with his partner; who eventually sees you as a confidant and a friend. Clashes have been part of the journey and, god-willing or by grace, the three of us have not veered completely off the tracks.

So somewhere, somehow, the prayers and tears and the hopes and joys worked. I have, for now, made it to a happy place, and I wish it for you, too. After all, a healthy, honest and loving relationship between a mother and son is one of the most potent guardians of well-being. I am happy when my sons are happy. That's a mother for you!

Tips for moms from other moms

Tear this out, try out the tips and write your own.

1. Love your son as a separate person and as a gift in your life.
2. Notice that your need for control hampers his expression.
3. Separate the venting of angry outbursts from communicating assertively.
4. A boy's strong life impulse (wilfulness) needs to be acknowledged as healthy. He needs a mission.
5. Aim for a mature young man, not a perfect teen.
6. Things (stuff) will not satisfy inner needs; only meaningful experiences and good relationships with living beings will.
7. Be aware of handing your boys over to popular culture; challenge yourself or him about following the pack.
8. If you keep your eye on the problem, you will continue to bump into it; broaden your perspective. Just make sure he knows the consequences of what he is doing.
9. Parenting is mostly about relationship-building.
10. Create zones that are free of pressure and conversations that are free of judgement.
11. Families who play together and pray together will stay together.
12. Your son's natural passion and creativity has to come from within him, not from within you.
13. Question whether a man's role is only to provide, protect, perform. He has a soul journey, too.
14. Plan holidays with nature contact – help boys reconnect to all their senses and have direct experiences.
15. Consider how your personal experiences around masculinity affect your parenting.
16. Know that he loves you and hears you. Action, and not always words, is often his language.
17. Remind him to access his 'sober second thoughts' and not only his animal instincts.
18. Remind yourself to re-focus attention on your own life – stop telescope-parenting.
19. Accept your limitations.
20. Accept that he will not tell you everything; secrets are part of being a teenager.
21. Set reasonable limits and clear boundaries. Allow him freedom within these limits.
22. Never stop telling your son that you believe in him and love him.

Parent resources

South African helplines:
Adcock Ingram depression and anxiety helpline 0800 70 80 90
ADHD helpline 0800 55 44 33
Akeso psychiatric response unit 0861 435 787
Childline 08000 55 555
Destiny helpline for youth and students 0800 41 42 43
LifeLine: National counselling line 0861 322 322
        Stop gender violence 0800 150 150
        AIDS helpline 0800 012 322
Pharmadynamics police and trauma line 0800 20 50 26
Rape Crisis 021 447 9762
South African Depression and Anxiety Group (SADAG) 011 234 4837
SADAG suicide crisis helpline: 0800 567 567 or SMS 31393
Substance abuse helpline 0800 12 13 14 or SMS 32312

Online resources
Parent information and courses you can attend or complete online:
Keep Connected www.keepconnected.searchinstitute.org
Megan de Beyer www.megandebeyer.com
Nikki Bush www.nikkibush.com/talks/parenting/
Parenting Resources www.parenting-resources.com/systematic-training-effective-parenting.htm
Priceless Parenting www.pricelessparenting.com
Udemy Neuroscience for Parents www.udemy.com/course/neuroscience-and-parenting/

A Facebook support group:
The Village:
www.facebook.com/groups/1718861155110611/

Resources to keep you safe:
Mankind Project for Dads www.mkpau.org
People Opposing Women Abuse (POWA) www.powa.co.za
Rape Crisis www.rapecrisis.org.za
SaferSpaces www.saferspaces.org.za

Drug rehabilitation centres:
Akeso Behavioural Healthcare Group www.akeso.co.za
Bethesda Addictions Treatment Centre www.bethesda4recovery.com
Crossroads Recovery Centres www.crossroadsrecovery.co.za
Healing Wings www.healingwings.co.za
Houghton House Addiction Recovery Centres www.houghtonhouse.co.za
Oasis Recovery Centre www.oasisrecoverycentre.com
Recovery Centre at White River www.whiteriverrecovery.co.za
Toevlug Alcohol and Drug Dependence Centre www.toevlug.org

Mental health centres and information:
Crescent Clinic www.crescentclinic.com
Life Healthcare www.lifehealthcare.co.za
SA Federation for Mental Health www.safmh.org.za

Free family counselling:
Families South Africa www.famsa.org.za

Make a list of your local resources

Every parent needs expert help that they can trust. Write in the numbers or e-mail addresses of your locals:

My doctor:
Closest hospital:
Allergy clinic:
My dermatologist:
A counselling centre:
An educational psychologist:
Family counsellor:
Tutorial services:
Au pair services:
Lift scheme:
Closest volunteer scheme:
Police child services:
Teen helpline:

Do email me at megan@megandebeyer.co.uk or check out my website for further information: www.megandebeyer.com.

Acknowledgements

Thank you to all the mothers and parents who attended my workshops over the past twelve years. It's your questions that are answered in this book. I also acknowledge all the schools in the UK, California and Australia who trusted me, as a foreign psychologist, to impart my learnings to parents.

A special thanks to Dr Jason Bantjes and Liz King at Bishops (Cape Town); Tim Jarvis at Michaelhouse (KwaZulu-Natal); and Ray Swan at Brighton Grammar School (Melbourne), who have promoted and supported my work.

Gratitude to Sarah Bullen, my South African agent who helped me kick-start this book. The editors have been essential: Ronel Richter-Herbert at Penguin Random House for her edits and support, and Lori Cohen for a last-minute read-through.

Thanks to Nadine Rubin of Highspot, my literary agent in New Zealand and Australia, who has plans for an audiobook, book tours and publishing my book in Australia.

A special thank you to Vanessa Raphaely for expecting the best of me.

My warmest gratitude to my partner Simon, my sister Carolyn, and my sons, James and Jo, for their loving support and encouragement. Without them this book would not have made it into your hands.